To Katy
in love + Light

The funny business of enlightenment

By

Nick Richardson

Dedication

For Sam and Jim who make me proud every day

Acknowledgments
Special thanks go to

Dilly, Sam and Jim. None of this would have happened without the love and support of Mum, Dad and Maxine. Thanks to Jacky and John Newcomb for the hours of help and advice and the well aimed kicks up the backside. To Helen and Vince for the many lifetimes of friendship together. To Eve for being a true friend and inspiration. To Lucy and Nancy for being two of the purest souls I know. To Isobel Hosie for her editorial skills. Special thanks go to the Kitt family and the Lloyd family. Many thanks go to Peter Adams, friend and Brother and to Ajda Vucicevic at LBA for her help.

This book is also dedicated to the memory of Ronald Gerald Hill.

And finally; Particular thanks go to Bruce Springsteen and all members of the E Street Band, on both sides of life, for the constant inspiration.

Introduction

As a small child I often pondered on life's big questions. Why are we here? What is the meaning of life? What happens when we die? Can chickens burp? So I asked my dad, but he didn't know much about chickens, so I enquired of him what happened when your life ends.

"Well, son" he said, "You're either cremated, which means you go up in a puff of smoke, or you're buried, which means you don't." He smiled at me, pleased to have satisfied my curiosity. I could imagine the conversation my sports-mad father was having with himself in his head. *'And dad has batted that tricky question away to the boundary for four runs.'* But I wasn't satisfied, this wasn't quite what I was after,

"I know all that, I persisted, "But what happens next? Where do you go?"
He looked puzzled and slightly lost; I had obviously bowled him a bouncer.

"Ah well, let's see now," he said, "You ...er, well I think that you er... it's...yes... you... hmmm." I'd stumped him. He resorted to the standard reply taught at *Parenting School.* "Ask your mother," he said.
Mum didn't really know either, even though she was always telling me that *'Mothers know everything!'*

I came across death first-hand when my sister's hamster died. 'Nipper' (She called him Nipper because that was his name) had been missing for three days after my sister had decided to give his cage its annual clean. She had taken Nipper and the cage into the bathroom, presuming that this would be a secure area with few hazards. She should have placed him in the bath of course, where he would never have escaped. He would have enjoyed slipping around on its enamel surface with his little feet; perhaps he might even have practiced a few *hamsters-on-ice* type moves. But no, she put him on the floor where he promptly made a break for freedom by disappearing behind the bath and refusing to come out. Even his favourite food didn't tempt him, which according to my sister was Weetabix covered in Angel Delight (which by some bizarre coincidence happened to be her favourite as well).

Three days later father found Nipper, even though he wasn't looking for him. Dad had gone into the garage to fetch a watering can so that he could refresh the weeds in our garden. After filling it to the brim he took it outside, but then wondered why it wouldn't pour. Looking inside he found the reason – Nipper was floating on his back with his little feet in the air, blocking the spout. He wasn't doing the backstroke, and wouldn't *ever* be doing anything again. My dad refused to give him the kiss of life, for fear of blowing him up to the size of a beach ball. My sister was heartbroken. First David Cassidy had left The Partridge Family and now this.

It wasn't a big funeral. Just an old shoebox buried under the silver birch tree in the garden, with two wooden lolly-sticks stapled together in the shape of a cross, the word 'Nipper' scrawled across them in shaky felt-tip pen.

It still made me wonder where he went though. Was that it? Was he now going to rot down and help the flowers grow or had he gone to heaven? And what *was* heaven anyway?

I asked my granddad. After all he was quite old, and therefore supposedly 'wise,' but he didn't know either. However, he did know how to make me a catapult out of an old T.V. aerial, so that was all right. Looking back, I nearly brought Granddad to the brink of death on numerous occasions. He had worked 'down the pit' all his life and had lungs full of coal dust. He would cough at the drop of a hat. I found out that if I said, "Salty Bacon, Granddad," to him, it would bring on a most satisfying coughing fit. His eyes would nearly burst from his head as his poor body was rocked by volcanic spasms as his chest tried to clear itself of decade's worth of coal dust. Eventually, after 20 minutes of furious hacking, he would sit back in the chair, panting and red in the face, wiping his teary eyes with a hanky. I was only seven years old and watched these fits with a mixture of fascination and sheer terror. I wondered what would happen if he slipped off this mortal coil right in front of my eyes. Would I get the blame? Was there any way I could shift the blame onto my sister? Luckily these seizures never proved fatal. Whenever I did question my granddad about death, he would just smile sweetly, shrug his shoulders and give a look of tired resignation; it was the same expression he had when my grandmother said she was making fruit cake...again!

By the time I was 10, my beloved granddad had passed away. I missed him terribly and I couldn't get my head around the fact that *that was it*. All finished; gone forever. What was the point? I knew his body had given up, but what of the man inside it? Where had *he* gone? I reasoned that once something was *made*, once it *existed* – it couldn't suddenly *no longer exist* or be *unmade*. That didn't make sense. Surely it just changed form and became something else. But what was that *something else*? I realised that I was going to have to find out for myself. I read anything I could find on the subject, and such material was quite uncommon back then. When I came across rare books in the library I soon became engrossed. My parents worried that I had a morbid fascination with death, but as the years rolled by, I realised that I had a fascination with LIFE – because *YOU DON'T DIE*. Life carries on after death, albeit in another form.

Thirty-Five years on, I am still learning. The death of my granddad, and that little hamster's demise have inadvertently led me on a wonderful journey of discovery about life, death, reincarnation, quantum physics, metaphysics, the concept of reality and much more.

Years later, I was told about a remarkable incident. Two days before my granddad's funeral, my mother was alone in the kitchen making me 'egg-in-a-cup' and whistling *Rhinestone Cowboy*, when she felt a distinct presence behind her. Walking towards her, through a wall, were her long-dead grandparents. Unlike the popular image given in cartoons, they weren't see-through or covered in a white sheet, carrying chains and going ooOO! They were as real and solid as when they had lived on this side of life. Remarkably, she wasn't alarmed or frightened by this (nothing defeats a British trained nurse!)

"Oh hello." she said, just stopping short of asking them if they would like a nice cup of tea. "What are you doing here?"

"It's okay," they said calmly, "we've come to take your dad. He's coming home with us." They smiled, turned and walked back the way they had come. Mother carried on with her chores as if nothing unusual had happened. She never mentioned this incident to me until I was an adult. I wondered why she hadn't told me at the time, given that I was always asking awkward questions. Perhaps she thought she was protecting me, and believed that I would have been scared by the incident – after all, I was a timid child. I always had to watch Scooby-Doo from behind the sofa, and don't get me started on Dr Who – it frightened the pants off me. I was told that Daleks came out of the household plug sockets, obviously a ploy to stop me getting electrocuted. I still hate the programme. My two sons love it, but I have to leave the room every time it comes on.

Maybe my mother wasn't protecting me at all, maybe she was afraid of ridicule, worried that people would think she was mad for claiming to have seen two ghosts; this was the 1970s and people weren't as open as they are today. There were no magazines on the subject and no Internet for communicating global phenomena or paranormal happenings.

Thankfully, research is now shared and experiences are published. We have more information and we realise we aren't alone, mad or foolish after all. My parents however, often claim that I still fall into the last two categories.

For the last 21 years, I feel as if I've been leading a double life. At weekends I earn my living by running my own large, indoor market unit in Cornwall, specialising in watches, batteries and watch straps, and during the week I have been on a long and strange spiritual journey; a search for enlightenment, if you like. Only working two days a week has enabled me to explore my life-long obsession with all things metaphysical. I spend half my time with my head in the clouds, investigating such diverse subjects as reincarnation, life after death or spirit guides, and then each weekend I am bought back down to earth by the random nature of my 'normal' everyday life, and my feet are planted firmly back on the ground once more.

Some of the more outlandish concepts that I studied took years to formulate properly in my head before I could accept them as plausible, and the more answers I found, the bigger the questions became. Underpinning this journey was my relationship and interaction with the diverse mix of characters that I have met through my work life, and they have served to show me the inter-connectedness of all aspects of my life. The Universe has a strange way of working; it throws up some incredible encounters and bizarre situations in its attempt to present you with the opportunities you need in order to learn your life lessons. They can arise in the strangest of ways and under the most bizarre of circumstances.

Life is a journey with lots of twists and turns, steep learning curves and easy straights, a few exiting downhill rides, and the occasional free-fall demon drop! If you are just setting out on your own journey I hope this book is of some value to you and will keep you company. If you are already on your journey, then maybe we can walk together for a while. It should be a laugh.

***

"I once spent the night with Shirley MacLaine." Quite a boast: after all, she is an Academy Award winning actress and bestselling writer; but then, Jack Bell was the king of the idle boast. "I played football with Len Shackleton at school."

Len Shackleton was one of football's greats. He played for Sunderland, Newcastle and England. Jack would turn any conversation into an opportunity to boast about who he knew personally. No matter what the subject, Jack would find a way in. Food, for example. "He liked a bit of black pudding did Len," would be his tenuous link, and his way of introducing us into 'Jack's world.' And once you were in Jack's kingdom, there was no escape.

He was a 'professional', straight-talking, 'a spade's a spade' Yorkshireman. Most of his conversations started with, "Now don't get me wrong but..." followed by a tirade of his own particular wisdom, which he shared with you whether you wanted to hear it or not.

Jack's boast of spending the night with Shirley MacLaine might have rendered itself more believable had it not been for his grotesque appearance. He was one of the scruffiest men I have ever seen. (And this isn't an idle boast – believe me!) Although well into his late 70's, his hair was still a muddy shade of brown, but so greasy that it stuck to his scalp in one congealed mass. Huge lumps of dandruff stood defiantly atop this goo, in a similar way to flaked almonds sitting proudly on a chocolate trifle. He wore enormous black-rimmed glasses that sat lopsided on his face and left one eye leering at you over the top of the smeary lenses. These were held together with green parcel tape, so too I believe was Jack. I never saw him in a change of clothes. Through summer and winter he wore a dirty, three-quarter length Mac over a garishly checked tweed jacket, the lapels of which had the wingspan of an albatross. His aged nylon shirt would, at one time, have been bright yellow, but was now a pale 'old man's wee' shade of its former self. The collar was so worn that it appeared he had two dishcloths hanging limply around his neck. The splash-stained gusset of his brown trousers hung midway between his knees. He never wore shoes, only plimsolls, and these were seriously worn away on one side. They gave Jack the appearance of walking sideways up a hill, as he shuffled his way behind my counter. Jack never required a new watch or a fresh battery; he only required some conversation and nearly all of it was his. Quite frankly he looked like he'd been run over – and the skid marks were evident all over his body.

He had obviously been taught at an early age that toothpaste was highly toxic; his teeth were so yellow they appeared to be coated in egg-yolk. When he talked he dribbled and spat at the same time. Jack had a withered arm, his right one being half the size of his left. He held it flaccidly from his body in the same manner that a chicken holds a bad foot. He was smelly, rude, arrogant, intriguing, knowledgeable, opinionated, argumentative, intelligent, captivating and infuriating... and I thought the world of him.

"Did I ever tell you about the time I worked with Tom Jones?" Jack made himself comfortable on one of my high work stools. This would indicate that he was staying for the afternoon, no matter how busy I was with genuine customers. "Aye, I played on one of his records, you know."

I raised one eyebrow. "Really Jack? You do surprise me." I replied, trying not to sound too sceptical. Of course, I had no idea at that moment, how totally astounded I was going to be. 'Never judge a book by its cover' was a life lesson I was going to have to learn...

***

Chapter 1
KEEP TAKING THE TABLETS

'I'm breaking through, I'm bending spoons,
I'm keeping flowers in full bloom,
I'm looking for answers from the great beyond.'

REM

It was a sight to behold: the lady, dancing on her own in the middle of the crowded hotel ballroom, was wearing a pink knitted balaclava and waving a child's plastic light-sabre. It was a strange dance routine. A sort of Morris-dance-meets-Star-wars with choreography taken from *Crouching Tiger, Hidden Dragon*. Not an uncommon occurrence at a New Age, Mind, Body and Spirit Festival – Home of the Free Spirit. The way she was moving suggested the spirits might not have been free, but certainly very cheap...

The crowd gazed at the lady with a mixture of looks. Some looked amused, most looked baffled, but a few seemed to be thoroughly enjoying it. I must admit my first thought was, 'what a loony, that's not normal.' My second thought was, 'so what?' Who am I to say what's normal? Who suddenly made *me* so important?'

Her message, if there was one, was totally lost on me. But did there need to be a message? Perhaps she just got pleasure from doing it and there was no higher reason than that. She certainly appeared to be enjoying herself.

Can you imagine how dull and boring life would be if we were all the same? Think of life without diversity, without difference, without anything to challenge our conceptions of what is normal. You would never need to travel abroad or experience different cultures, what a grey world that would be. Heaven forbid - we'd all look like politicians.

I started to admire the lady. It takes a lot of guts (or in my case, a lot of beer) to get up in front of people and dance alone. If I ever head for the dance floor at a wedding, my sons look on in horror.

In all seriousness, though, how often have *you* been ridiculed for saying what you believe in? It's amazing how aggressive some people become when you tell them, for example, that you believe in life-after-death or reincarnation. I've been laughed at many times by people when I tell them that I believe that I am intrinsically a soul inhabiting a body. The usual comment is *'keep taking the tablets.'* The most vehement are normally those who have never even thought about the subject of spirituality, the sheep who stay safely amongst the flock. Their philosophy is: *If you don't understand someone, hate them for it.*

The festival my wife, Dilly, and I were attending is held every year in a large hotel in a coastal town near to our home. The four-day event offers all manner of talks, workshops, demonstrations and the opportunity to purchase items as diverse as diving-rods and clip-on fairy wings. We walked around the stalls set up throughout the various rooms in the hotel. Many of them were selling jewellery. This ranged from beautiful hand-worked silver, inlaid with semi-precious stones, to lengths of old fuse wire with pre-sucked cough-sweets hanging from them.

There is always a problem at shows like this; sorting out the plausible from the downright unlikely. One man had welded together a collection of old copper piping, obviously gleaned from building sites and skips. He had formed it into a strange hexagonal shape, which looked like a battered greenhouse missing all its glass. He had the audacity to charge people £25 to sit inside it for half an hour, claiming this was their ticket to gaining some kind of astral wisdom. At the other extreme was the most wonderful bookstall. Every subject you could ever wish to study was represented: Healing, Afterlife Communication, Metaphysics, Knights Templars, Freemasonry and Quantum Theory, to name but a few. It was an antidote to some of the more outrageous stalls, and a reminder that sometimes you have to search to find the truth. Sitting down for 30 minutes under some old pipes and expecting the answer to the universe is unrealistic. You have a responsibility to do some of the groundwork yourself. The joy of a journey is in the experiences along the way, and not necessarily in reaching your destination. Knowledge comes through experience and learning, through trying different things and evaluating the results. We'd all like a magic wand to wave whenever we feel the need, but what would be the point in having all the answers given to us if we didn't have to strive in some way to get them; and by strive, I don't mean struggle. Knowledge should come through joy and happiness. It isn't bestowed upon us as a reward for going through pain or suffering, as some organised religions would have us believe. Enlightenment is more likely to come through experiencing moments of pleasure and laughter, than from flaying yourself with birch twigs or wearing a hair shirt.

As we walked around, a duo took the stage with a vast array of drums. They started playing, and within moments all eyes were on them. The beat was infectious; a loud, raucous and unapologetic thump, with the vibration of the sound hitting you with a 'thwack' in the solar plexus; an ancient and earthy, natural sound, unadulterated by electronic amplification. Within minutes, people were clapping in time, stamping their feet and dancing, united in a shared moment of abandonment. As the beat got faster, your heart seemed to travel with it and your soul seems to awaken as if from a deep sleep. One of the duo began to chant loudly, like a Native American, it made the hairs on your neck stand up. Perhaps it was unlocking a primeval memory.

After all, this was how people gathered together in communities thousands of years ago; this is what bound them together and was important to them; this is what we did before television, and it was certainly more entertaining than old re-runs of the *Rockford Files*.

Trade seemed brisk for a number of businesses, namely tarot readers and people offering healing. Dilly spotted someone taking Aura Photographs and walked towards them."Why don't you have your aura photographed?" she suggested. I glanced across at the equipment. It was slightly more intimidating than an electric chair. Two metal boxes were placed either side of a seat. They had chrome plates on the top where you placed your hands, Protruding from the rear were lengths of multicoloured wire, which ran to the back of a large camera mounted onto a tripod.

"Does it hurt?" I asked bravely.

"Of course it doesn't, you big baby," Dilly replied, " It captures the coloured energy field around your body. Some people call it '*Kirlian*' photography after the man who discovered it."

"Nobody has a name like '*Kirlian Photography*,'" I said.

"Every living thing has an aura," she continued, ignoring me. "It's a snap-shot of the life-force within you"

The life force within my wife then pushed me violently in the back towards the chair; I stumbled and fell into place.

"How much is it?"

"Twenty five pounds" said the man.

"How much?" I choked, "I could get Lord Lichfield for that!" This was the Cornishman in me coming out.

Dilly gave me a withering look. I put it in my pocket for later.

I placed my hands on the two metal boxes. In my mind I decided I would make a run for it if anyone offered me a black hood to wear, or a damp sponge for the top of my head. I settled back, took a deep breath and waited for the inevitable jolt. In that moment I realised I was too young to die. There was so much I hadn't done. So many ambitions left to fulfil. I wanted to see my sons winning the *Ashes* for England, ride naked through Penzance on a Triumph Bonneville, style Anne Widdicomb's hair and go on a steam train in an anorak. All these worthwhile endeavours left unfulfilled, and here I was, about to be fried to a crisp.

"All finished," said the man behind the camera, shaking me out of my reverie.

"Never felt a thing," I said, rising from the chair like a phoenix from the flames."Nothing to it!"

The actual photograph took about 5 minutes to develop. I sat down next to a lady who interpreted the picture for me. As she peeled off the protective paper a wonderful spectrum of colours was revealed. Smokey, cloudy hews, and in the middle of it all was *me*.

"As you look at the photo," the lady explained, "the colours on the right are entering your aura, and those on the left are leaving."

It was similar to a psychic reading (except that the lady's name wasn't Doris). She talked about the colours that were leaving my aura as events that had happened in the last two months. She was totally accurate. She described how the aura soaks up energy from the body; for instance, if you have been ill, it will show up in the colouring. It can also highlight positive traits, such as having a certain talent. I have a certain talent for impersonating Billy Connolly, but he didn't show up in my aura.

I am a little colour-blind, and so to me, the different shades appeared rather mixed up, rather like a chicken tikka-masala that had been accidentally dropped on to a highly patterned carpet. Luckily the patient lady took me through each colour. An interesting swirl of yellow was entering my aura from the right. Did this mean custard for tea? Apparently not. She felt this meant I could be doing something creative in the near future. Could adding bananas to custard be classed as creative, I wondered?

"It could be painting," she continued, "but I feel it's more likely to be writing."

The deeper shades on the other side of the picture gave me the appearance of having had a lopsided blue rinse, a sort of 'wind-swept Marge Simpson' look. My expert interpreter enlightened me.

"Blue can indicate having found your life's vocation," she said, "definitely communication."

"You need to try and do some writing," she urged, "Experiment a bit. I think you will find that the more you do it the easier it becomes. It's a bit like turning on a tap and letting it flow."

So that's what I did. I started to write about anything and everything. I did it just for *me*. I wrote on the backs of receipts, on my shirt cuffs, up my arm and on my wife's best tablecloth. It's a wonderfully freeing experience, doing something totally for *yourself*. It can be anything – singing, poetry, drumming or even playing the Patagonian nose flute, (although this can be tricky if you have a heavy cold.) Why not try it? You don't have to explain or justify it to anybody else - make it just for you.

After lunch, we had a workshop booked. It was titled 'Working with Angels,' which I thought might require me to dress up as a nurse, but no, it was an introduction into utilizing angelic forces. I was the only man in a room of 40 women. The lady giving the talk spoke at length about astral beings and such like, but if I'm honest, I have to say it left me cold. My mind started to wander and I think at one point

I may even have nodded off. Unexpectedly though, things suddenly became more entertaining. The teacher started to sing. It wasn't anything from the charts, though; she started to sing in a strange, falsetto voice, complete with a false vibrato. There were no words, just lots of ooohing and ahhhing. She sounded like an amateur soprano strolling over broken glass. She walked amongst the class with her voice rising and falling like a runaway rollercoaster. This was more like it, I thought. My ears began to ring. As I looked around, I noticed a few other people who also found it amusing, including Dilly, who I dared not look at. Perhaps Angels is a 'woman's thing', because I noticed the majority of the ladies in the room were sitting with their eyes closed and heads bowed as if in prayer or meditation. The warbling continued for a further 10 minutes, although it felt longer, and then the lady walked around passing on messages from the great beyond to each person in turn. When my turn came I wasn't expecting any sharing of astral wisdom. "They're putting a book in your lap," she said. I was quite taken aback at this. "It's not a book you are reading," she added, "it is a book you are to write." My brain was suddenly a-whir. Once again I had made up my mind about this whole episode within seconds of entering the room, only to be proved wrong it would seem, as writing was now high on my agenda. They say 'it takes all sorts,' and the message obviously still got through despite the fact that I found it comical. I must admit it made me question my attitude towards other people, although with hand on heart, if I was in the same situation again, I couldn't promise not to chuckle – but maybe that's the point, I get the message eventually, and more often than not, I can laugh and enjoy the journey along the way.

Later that evening I was discussing the day with our 5-year-old son, Jim. I tried to explain to him about auras, energy, spirituality and ultimately God. He sat quietly for a moment.

"I've seen God," he said.

I was amazed. "Have you?" I asked, "What does He look like?"

"Well, He's orange and He's got a square head."

***

"I owe you an apology." Malcolm said as he walked across the isle from his counter to mine, with a contrite look on his face.

"What on earth for?" I asked wondering why he looked so apprehensive. Had he perhaps inadvertently backed his car into mine? Or let slip to the market manager that it was me who surreptitiously kept placing peculiar items up for sale on a vacant pitch? These included half a digestive biscuit with a large For Sale sign declaring 'one careful owner and guaranteed for two years against leakage and foul-pest – £18 apply at Market Office.' Or the punctured football For Sale at £22.50 with a sign saying 'Company Gone Burst Due to Over Inflation.' I desperately hoped he hadn't split on me because I had just had a miraculous find in a skip; the bottom half of a tailors dummy and I was in the process of working out a cunning plan for the best way to advertise it. But no it was none of these things.

"I need to apologise for introducing Jack Bell to you," he said. Jack and Malcolm had known each other for many years, and initially Jack would visit the market especially to see him, but had inadvertently become attached to me also. "I hope he hasn't made a nuisance of himself."

"You're joking!" I said quickly, not wanting Malcolm to worry. "He's marvellous; I've never met a character like him. To be quite honest he fascinates me."

"Has he told you he spent the night with Shirley MacLaine?"

"You bet he has," I said, laughing, "And a few more tales besides – where does he get these fantasies from?"

"They're all true." He stated emphatically. There was a moment's silence between us as he looked me straight in the eyes, waiting to see how this news would register in them. I knew Malcolm wouldn't lie, and he wasn't the type to play tricks either. He must have realised by my confused expression that I was struggling to comprehend this shock revelation. I'm willing to believe in all sorts of things: UFO's, life on Mars, Elvis is still alive and running a kebab shop in Redruth; but Jack Bell and Shirley MacLaine? I couldn't believe it. Think of his appearance, he lived in a caravan and smelt of cheese.

"Balls," I said "No way."

Malcolm was very kind. He closed his eyes and nodded in a friendly understanding kind of way. He took on the air of a kindly grandpa about to inform you he's just run over your pet rabbit with his lawnmower. He placed a hand on my shoulder, "I know its hard son," he said, "But I swear to you it is true." Malcolm then filled me in on all his dealings with Jack Bell.

After the war, Jack became one of the most respected musicians in Britain; he played trumpet in some of the country's biggest dance and jazz bands, and toured widely with Maynard Ferguson. (Whom he later formed a company with) He was great friends with the likes of Kenny Baker, Sid Lawrence and Stan Kenton. At the time, these men were the gods of their day, equivalent to any of today's super-bands. He played on hundreds of records, including the famous Tom Jones hit; 'It's Not Unusual' He also appeared on TV theme tunes, such as The Muppets and Match of the Day, and many others.

Malcolm revealed that he too at one time had considered Jack's stories fictional. They worked together occasionally in their capacity as members of a business federation, which meant attending meetings throughout the country. One day, while travelling through Nottingham together, they were passing a large theatre advertising that the Ken Macintosh Band were appearing.

"I know him," said Jack.

Malcolm looked to the heavens, "Yes, I'm sure you do." he said flatly.

"You don't believe me, do you? Right I'll show you." With a screech of tyres, Jack pulled the car over onto the pavement, right outside the front steps of the theatre. "Come on you," he said, dragging Malcolm out of the passenger seat by his coat collar. He marched him to the top

of the steps and stood rapping loudly and persistently on the main doors until eventually they were opened by a member of staff.

"I'm afraid we're close..."

"Shurrup and listen," Jack said swiftly, cutting off the man in mid sentence. "Go inside and tell Ken Macintosh that Jack Bell is here to see him. Quick man, it's urgent." This was said with such authority that the man turned tail and set off at a sprint. Five minutes later the door opened and a grinning Ken Macintosh strolled out.

"Hey, Jack Bell," he called, his arm stretched out to offer a handshake, "It's great to see you again, how are you?"

"Never mind that," said Jack, waving away the outstretched hand. He shoved Malcolm in the back; propelling him smartly forward, "Tell this jumped- up little bugger that you know me, will you!"

Jack arrived later that afternoon, but he wasn't his usual ebullient self. He seemed downcast and chastened.

"Are you all right Jack?" I asked.

"Yes, not bad lad. I've just been to a funeral." he replied. I wondered which world leader had died without my knowing. "We've just buried my good pal Kenny Baker." Not for the first time, a pang of guilt rushed through me. "I had the honour of walking behind his coffin and carrying his

MBE on a cushion." His sad eyes looked into mine for a moment. "Won't be long until you need to start worrying about that," he said.

Did he know something I didn't? Surely Nostradamus wasn't an old friend as well...

***

Chapter 2

THINKING OUTSIDE THE BOX

'I hope you die before me,

Because I don't want you singing at my funeral'

Spike Milligan to Sir Harry Secombe

As I get older, the subject of death and dying seems to be creeping into my life in none too subtle ways; Jack's comment being the least subtle of all. A few years ago I passed my forty-fifth birthday, waved it goodbye, and watched it disappear in the rear view mirror of life at a terrifying pace. For years my conversations would revolve around the latest happenings in the world of sport or music, but latterly it seems as if I am having never ending discourse with people in grey suits talking endlessly about mortgages, wills, pensions, health checks and insurance policies, and I seem to be asked about funeral arrangements with more regularity than I am comfortable with. It's not something that takes up a lot of my time, but a recent health scare did make me think a bit more about the subject.

After all, you never know when your number might be up. I might go out tomorrow and get flattened by a steamroller. I suppose if a steamroller did flatten me, at least I could be buried in a jiffy-bag and save money on a coffin. My granny spent years worrying that I might get hit by a bus and not be wearing clean underwear. It didn't matter that my brain might have been squeezed out through my ears by the front wheels of a double-decker, so long as my Littlewoods paisley Y-fronts were minty-fresh. In fact the last thing she said to me before she died was, "Nick, always wear clean underpants, and always ALWAYS keep your receipts!"

There are any number of ways that I might slip off this mortal coil. Living in Cornwall the chances are I'll either choke to death on a huge pasty or more likely drown from my thoroughly inept attempts at surfing. I know of a friend of a friend who recently drank himself to death. In one session he put away so much beer that he passed out, was rushed to hospital and physically died, but was luckily resuscitated. His reaction to this episode was a revelation. He felt he'd been given another chance, a new beginning, he had been re-born. He decided to start his life over again from the year zero. On the anniversary of his 'close call' he had a first birthday party and everyone bought him cuddly toys and sleepy-suits. This is now an annual tradition and this man of 40 is fast approaching his 5th birthday. He's hoping for a new bike!

So what happens when you die? I know you go stiff then start to smell a bit funny, but what then? Is there anything beyond the grave? Having studied the subject for over half my life, I'm convinced that death isn't the end; in fact the opposite is true, it's the beginning. Every year there are hundreds of cases world-wide of people who 'die' but are then bought back to life to tell their stories, (otherwise known as a Near Death Experience) I'm sure you are all familiar with the 'tunnel-of-light' and 'meeting-with-loved-ones' scenario. There is a theory that these experiences are all a result of certain chemicals flooding the brain at the point of death. But what about the dozens of cases of people who are resuscitated and can then tell you very clearly and succinctly everything that has occurred since the moment of their supposed passing? They float out of their bodies and hover over the scene and can repeat accurately what was said to individuals at the place of an accident or to hospital workers or even to anxious relatives. Their lifeless body might be hooked up to all the latest medical equipment that states categorically that there is no sign of life, and yet the supposedly dead person is observing all this. Afterwards they can tell you with startling precision what medical staff have written down and even in some cases what has been discussed in a different room with total accuracy. Later independent witnesses can frequently corroborate this evidence.

How could they know these things unless some part of our consciousness carries-on after we die? After all it is a scientific fact that energy doesn't die, it just changes form. Thought is pure energy, but the brain doesn't create it.

Thought is created elsewhere and the brain is a convenient host to enable that thought to become recognised. If energy never dies, where does it go to once the host can no longer accommodate it? Near Death Experiences would suggest that it continues to retain a degree of consciousness, but in a different dimension.

Imagine your brain is like a radio. You look in the back and it's a jumble of circuit boards and interconnecting wires, but it's just a useless lump of plastic and metal without the invisible radio waves that are beamed across the atmosphere. Turn the machine on (i.e. provide it with energy) and it bursts into life and offers entertainment, information and communication. But the radio itself doesn't create these programmes, they originate elsewhere. Turn the radio off and it becomes lifeless and inert, but the signal is still being broadcast. It hasn't gone away; you just don't hear it anymore. However, it's still available to those who can 'tune into' the correct frequency. I'm sure this is how mediums work; they twiddle their knob and change the frequency of their thought patterns and brainwaves and, hey presto! A direct line to Spirit FM, broadcasting 24/7 with no crappy adverts.

With death being a certainty for us all, I am surprised that big businesses have never gone into the lucrative funeral market; it's guaranteed that they would never be short of work and they could sponsor all aspects of the service:

This funeral is bought to you in association with Mr Whoopsie's Ice-cream Parlour – A real taste of heaven.

Vicars could get in on the act and make themselves some spare cash.

Ashes to ashes, dust to dust - can now all be removed with the new super-suction bag-less vacuum cleaner, for only £79.99, at all good hardware stores.

Even the animal kingdom needn't feel left out.

Pooch Pet Cemeteries- It's a dog's life-or at least it was!

In these contentious days of mass litigation, and our seemingly ever increasing obsession with suing people, I am amazed that funeral parlours don't display legal disclaimers:

Warning

Being cremated could seriously affect you health and render your life insurance policy inactive. We take no responsibility for death or injury, how-so-ever caused whilst you are on these premises. If, however, your death is caused away from these premises we will gladly welcome you back with open arms and open chequebook.

Remember: YOUR LOSS IS OUR GAIN

A friend of mine attended a funeral recently where the man in question had suffered a long illness. He had taken the time to tie up all the loose ends in his life and spent many happy hours speaking to family and friends. He even went to the trouble of organising the whole of his funeral himself and insisted that it be done to his specifications.

He was a very popular man, and so when the day of his funeral came the church was filled with hundreds of friends and relatives. He'd always been known as a bit of a joker and at the end of the service the vicar announced that he had something further to say. He told the congregation that it was the deceased's wish that he read out a letter to them."I will miss you all." the vicar began, "Thank you for your friendship and support throughout my lifetime. I have been lucky to have lived my whole life in a village that I love; surrounded by the best friends a man could wish for. I have known a lot of you here today since our schooldays, and that is why I have left £200 behind the bar in the pub and want you all to go over there and have a final drink on me." This raised a number of smiles and a lot of appreciative comments. "All that is," the vicar continued "Except my best mate Norman Bootle, who is the tightest bugger that ever walked the earth and never bought a round in his life!"

The church erupted, with Mr Bootle apparently laughing the loudest. Knowing the Cornish sense of humour, I would imagine that the congregation were true to the deceased mans wishes and made Mr Bootle pay for his own booze whilst they all got happily inebriated. I bet his best friend was looking down from above and thinking 'he who laughs last'. Now *that* is leaving with style.

I'm certain that Mr Bootle wasn't offended and would have been the first to say, "Best funeral I've ever been to." This statement, of course, is always said out of respect and meant as a compliment. It means that the service offered a true reflection of the person that it honoured. It captured some of the essence of the deceased and served as a tribute to their memory. I even heard wild applause after the eulogy at the last funeral I attended. It was in the heart of the 'Black Country' in the West Midlands and the gentleman who read the eulogy had the broadest accent imaginable. The deceased was famous for having a really strong accent and this speech honoured that fact. It was full of eloquence, humour and respect and perfectly formulated into words what the congregation were feeling in their hearts. Everyone in the Chapel was there out of love for the deceased and this speech was a reflection of that love. When he finished, the applause was spontaneous, but it wasn't for him; it was for what he had said, and I know for a fact that it offered huge comfort and solace to the grieving family.

Even though, on the whole, funerals are quite sad occasions, there are sometimes some wonderfully humorous cameo performances. I had been asked by one family if I would be kind enough to offer a lift to a very elderly uncle. He was well into his nineties and the spring in his step looked as if it could do with a drop of oil. As we pulled up outside the Crematorium he turned to me and nodded his head towards it, "Hardly worth me going home is it?" he said with a wink.

Being a bit of a show off, I quite fancy the sound of a Viking funeral. A coffin in the shape of a long-ship would be good. It could be set alight and floated out on the nearest boating lake. I suppose at some time I am going to have to pick out a coffin for myself, what a strange thought that is. I've never fancied the idea of having an open casket; you know the type I mean, where there's a sort of sunroof revealing the deceased's head, the cabriolet of the coffin world you might say. Apparently the place to go if you require a really far-out coffin is Ghana in Africa. Here they custom build coffins that reflect your career or hobbies. They are highly decorated and very life-like. For example, if you were a cobbler you can be buried in a six-foot shoe complete with laces. Other options include beer bottles, chickens, televisions, three-seater sofas, racing cars - in fact virtually anything that you can think of is acceptable. I thought about Jack Bell; I bet he would love one in the shape of a trumpet. Although knowing Jack's luck, he would ask for one in the shape of a 'cornet' and end up being interred for eternity in a six foot ice cream cone. It begs the question though, what do you get buried in if you were an undertaker?

The Bo people of China are different again. They place their dead in conventional coffins but they don't bury them. They hang the coffins by ropes over cliffs and leave them there, suspended in mid air. Hundreds of boxes can be seen dangling precariously from sheer rock faces. Unless you are a committed mountaineer, I should imagine this makes it a bit tricky to leave flowers at the graveside. We aren't short of cliff faces down here in Cornwall, but I can't see the idea catching on. It would make a day at the beach a bit off-putting if there was a chance of a corpse falling onto your picnic.

Some countries don't bury their dead at all and leave the deceased exposed to the elements on a mountaintop. The local bird population soon makes short work of disposing of the remains. Once again I think this may struggle to become popular, even though Cornwall has a plethora of peckish seagulls. I must admit it would make a change from watching them mug unsuspecting tourists of their pasties.

The other option, of course, is a cremation. This allows for an assortment of options as to what you do with the ashes. They could be scattered somewhere of significance, or buried beneath a freshly planted tree, left on the mantelpiece in a fancy urn or even sealed in a rocket and blasted into space. The other option is to have your loved one's ashes converted into a diamond. In a miraculous process, the forces of nature that forge natural diamonds are recreated in laboratory conditions to produce genuine diamonds from human remains.

Cremated ashes contain carbon and this is the element used to make the diamond. When the carbon is heated to 3000 degrees it changes into graphite. This in turn is placed in a special chamber and subjected to enormous amounts of heat and pressure; something approaching 1000000 P.S.I. This causes the graphite to break down into individual atoms, then at a given temperature the carbon molecules come together to form a true diamond. What fascinates me about this process is the shape of the special chamber where all of this magical alchemy occurs. It is an octahedral; in other words, a four-sided pyramid with another pyramid attached at its base, mirror fashion. The octahedral is one of the five Platonic Solids, better known as 'the building blocks of life'. The others are the tetrahedron, the cube, the dodecahedron and the icosahedron. Together they form the blueprint of everything in creation, and are the geometrical building blocks of stars, galaxies, universes, our bodies, cells, DNA, plants, music and language – in short, 'all that is.'(This is, interestingly, another name for God.) Once you have your diamond, you can have it cut and shaped to your own design and then set into a piece of jewellery, bringing a whole new meaning to the term 'diamond geezer.' So ladies, it is now possible to have your loved one wrapped around your little finger for eternity.

Knowing that we live forever changes my view on how my funeral should be. I would like to think that it would be a celebration of my life. It would be nice if a few friends said some pleasant things about me, like how generous I was or how good a mate I had been. Although, it's a poor show when you have to die in order to get a compliment from your friends. I might even consider leaving a couple of quid behind the bar for them all to share a drink, and I stress 'A' drink! But really a funeral is also an opportunity for those left behind to find some closure. Of course there is always going to be a certain amount of pain involved in losing someone dear to you, no matter how old they may be, and to be honest funerals are very rarely a knees-up. Sometimes tragic circumstances make it impossible for the funeral to be anything other than harrowing. It can take a long time to come to terms with the loss of a loved one, but eventually you *do* have to come to terms. It's okay to be sad or distressed, and it's understandable to be shocked or angry and feel 'how dare you leave me alone!' But it is of the utmost importance to eventually realise you have to let them go. Not to forget, but to let them move on with their journey. If you don't, you become stuck as well. Other members of your family may find it hard to move on too and before you know it, more than one life has been destroyed;

many more have died somewhere inside themselves. The spirit person will be aware of this, and imagine the guilt they might feel, putting their loved ones through so much pain. It's your choice and your right to get through it and cope with it any way you see fit, but eventually we all have to move on. Remember, it's not goodbye forever, just for a while.

The real truth is that, 'We are as dead now as we ever will be.' Life is eternal. I know I will merely shift in consciousness. There's a good chance that I will attend my own funeral anyway and look down from the 'other side,' just to see who's bothered to turn up for the free sausage rolls and warm beer.

One thing is certain; I don't want any long faces at the service, so strictly no horses...

***

The elderly man who approached my sales counter walked with a farmer's gait, even though he didn't look strong enough to carry one. He waddled towards me with that strange bow-legged walk perfected by men who've spent their lives working the land. He had the obligatory flat cap perched on the back of his head, as if it was afraid to go too near his bright, ruddy face for fear of being incinerated by its red-hot heat. His trousers were pulled up to just below his nipples and fastened carelessly with red bailer twine. A frayed off-white vest peered cautiously from between a stained nylon shirt that had sweat patches the size of the Norfolk Broads. His trousers were tucked into odd socks that protruded from his enormous boots. The sole of one boot flapped loosely as he walked, looking like a fish gasping for air. The odd bluebottle flew wildly around his head, too scared to land for fear of catching something. The smell suggested he kept pigs; possibly in his bed...

"Do you replace watch badderies?" He said, in as thick a Cornish accent as I had ever heard.

I nodded; I couldn't quite find my voice.

He rolled back a ragged shirt cuff, and as the aged cloth was peeled back, bits fell to the floor as if an old parchment was being unfurled. With fingers the size of my legs, he began to unbuckle his watch. As it came loose, the hardened and decayed leather strap stayed in the shape of his wrist He placed it in front of me and I cast my eye over the back of the watch. It was covered in what appeared to be congealed marmite with a few human hairs sticking out of it. My nostrils gave a nervous twitch as the faint aroma of a medieval charnel house hit them. He reminded me of one of the extras from Michael Jackson's Thriller video.

"I think it's dead," he barked, as bits of breakfast shot out of his mouth towards me. Not unlike its owner I thought. "Only, I did get 'im wet." The only way this watch could get wet, was if it fell in a trough. I couldn't picture this man having showered or bathed since the war; I was intrigued.

"How did it get wet?" I asked, picking the offending item up carefully between my thumb and forefinger, as if handling a scorpion.

"I dropped 'im down the loo!" he spat. My fingers sprang apart and I released the offending item onto my countertop; I had a dreadful image of an unflushed toilet, and this man bending down elbow deep in the murky depths, sloshing around trying to find his lost timepiece.

"How on earth did you drop it down the loo?"

"Well now, it was like this..." he said leaning back on his heels and grabbing hold of his braces as if he were a college professor about to impart some great wisdom. "...I was washing me foot, when..."

"Whoa, whoa, stop a minute." I cut in, holding up my hand. *"You were washing your foot in the toilet?"*

"Yeah that's right," he said, looking at me with a puzzled expression that said 'doesn't everybody?' *"I was washing me foot because I've just had me gangrenous toe amputated and I can't bend down to wash 'im. So I sticks me foot in the loo, pulls the chain and gives 'im a good rinsing, only me foot got sucked round the bend, so I had to reach down to yank 'im out, and poop! Off came me watch."* He stood back and looked at me as if I was about 5 years old. *"Now can you do 'im or not?"* He snapped impatiently.

It took 3 hot hand washes and 5 squirts of anti-bacterial gel to remove the putrid stench from my hands.

***

Chapter 3

LIFE'S A SCREAM

Be silly, be honest, be kind.
Ralph Waldo Emerson.

I've never seen a ghost. I've *looked* like one many a time, but I've never actually set eyes on one. The only thing that goes bump in the night in our house is me, falling downstairs at 2 am trying to find the toilet, whilst still half asleep. I often wonder what my reaction would be if I did indeed meet one. Do they look like the ghosts on Scooby Doo? This is, of course, always 'old man Palmer' the owner of the amusement park, covered in an old sheet. I'd like to think I would be very adult and have 'a nice little chat' with it, but in truth, I dare say a change of underwear would be quickly needed.

I have various friends and family who have seen them. One, who worked as a security guard at an exhibition centre in Birmingham, swears that one of the major halls is haunted, and that an old monk has been seen on CCTV. Apparently none of the guards will patrol this particular spot at night. My sister worked in a hospice where ghosts were occasionally seen. One night her colleague followed a lady along a corridor. The lady turned and smiled, then walked into a storeroom. Thinking a visitor had taken a wrong turn;

she followed her. Once inside, she realised she had come in through the only door and that the storeroom was completely empty. The smiling lady had vanished into thin air! The poor nurse had to go home.

I knew one girl who had a classic poltergeist problem. She was fourteen years old at the time, a common age for such activity. The family had recently moved house and her bedroom was in a converted attic that was accessed via loft ladders. Every night the ladders would be pulled up into the room after her. Before going to bed she would carefully fold her clothes and place them neatly on the floor, but every morning when she awoke and went to get dressed, she discovered the clothes to be soaking wet, so wet in fact that she could wring them out. None of the floor around or beneath the clothes was wet and the carpet always remained dry. She moved her clothes to a different position each night, but the result was always the same. Before long other strange things started to occur. She awoke one morning to discover all her photograph albums strewn across the floor. Each picture had been removed from its transparent plastic housing and thrown randomly over the carpet. It wasn't long before pictures in frames suffered the same fate, only this time with the glass being smashed.

She was obviously petrified by this nightly violence and told her parents. They were convinced that she must be doing this herself in her sleep. She was adamant that she wasn't and so, for two nights she slept in her parents' room. There was nothing to report after the first night, and her parents tried to persuade her to go back to her own room for the second night. She refused and during that night her room was again trashed. There is no way she could have sneaked out of her parents' room and done this herself, as she couldn't reach the retractable loft ladders that would give her access to the attic. Two weeks later, the family put the house on the market and moved shortly afterwards. Luckily, the problem didn't follow them.

This case shares some similarities with a very famous paranormal happening that took place in London in the 1970s called the Enfield poltergeist. A single mother and her four children were the subject of intensive media scrutiny when the very strange goings on in their house was made public. The children were aged from 10 through to 12 years of age, with most of the activity being centred on a pair of twin girls. A team of psychic investigators were called in and witnessed some of the activity. Objects such as marbles and rocks were said to apport out of nowhere and were hurled across rooms as if by an unseen hand, and on closer examination were always said to be hot to the touch. Fires reportedly spontaneously ignited and then extinguished themselves; pools of water would be found lying on floors. On a number of occasions both people and furniture were levitated around the rooms. One of the more disturbing elements to the story was when one of the young girls started to channel messages from a discarnate entity called Bill. He claimed to have lived in the house before and had died there from a brain haemorrhage. The investigators did some research and discovered that a previous occupant had indeed died there from a brain haemorrhage and his name had been Bill. The family may have already known this of course, and there were obviously some suspicions of the whole thing being a hoax. However, some of the most compelling evidence came from people with no connection to the family. One of these was a serving policewoman, who signed an affidavit attesting to the fact that she had witnessed furniture being levitated and moved around the room. She examined the furniture for hidden wires or any other means of propulsion and found no signs of foul play. Photographers had problems with cameras suddenly not working inside the house and a BBC crew found their recording equipment to be faulty even though it had worked perfectly outside of the property. On closer examination they discovered the metal parts inside the apparatus were bent and damaged beyond all recognition. Needless to say that a full days recording had been mysteriously erased as well. In all, over thirty people claimed to have witnessed paranormal activity in the house. The psychic researchers were fully aware of the whole thing being seen as an elaborate hoax, and so invited in an independent scrutineer. She was a barrister called Mary Rose Barrington, and she cross examined the witnesses and cast her professional eye over the evidence and concluded that there were no grounds on which to suspect a conspiracy.

This all took place over thirty years ago and I cant help thinking that if this was to occur nowadays the family would have every 'Ghost Hunt' T.V. programme beating a path to their door in the hope of staging a 24 hour vigil. With the advent of digital technology, it would be so much easier to have the house under constant surveillance. These programmes, which have become very popular over recent years, are a strange mix of comedy and terror. The modus operandi of such shows is to kit out teams of paranormal investigators with night vision cameras and other electronic paraphernalia in the hope of capturing genuine psychic phenomena on film. They are then let loose in old castles, stately homes, derelict warehouses and pubs, in fact any location that would have graced an episode of Scooby Doo. And yes, I do believe an old Theme Park has been investigated, but to the best of my knowledge Old Man Palmer didn't make an appearance on the Ghost Train and say, "I would've gotten away with it if it wasn't for you pesky kids!"...Shame really.

Quite often the slightest creak from an old floorboard or random gurgle of ancient pipe-work can send the most skittish of investigators running for the nearest exit. I have to admit to a guilty voyeuristic pleasure in watching somebody being scared witless from the comfort and safety of my armchair. I particularly like the 'celebrity' episodes where I can watch well-known people from the world of soap operas and pop music being reduced to a quivering wreck at the sound of a mouse trumping or door slamming. A lot of these people may not have any particular interest or knowledge of the paranormal and so they can sometimes be extra jumpy, which makes for even better telly!

Most shows have a resident medium and a 'sceptical' parapsychologist, and for me, this is where the show gets interesting. Neither are told beforehand about the location to be investigated, therefore no prior research can be done. As the show progresses, the medium conveys any information that they are receiving as to relevant names, dates or significant incidents associated with the location. This can then be verified, or not, by later research, and on balance, I normally find the evidence given by the Psychic to be quite compelling. I find it perfectly feasible that throughout our lives we leave an 'energy imprint' attached to the fabric of space and time. I am sure that many old buildings are full of this residual energy, and it is this 'vibrational fingerprint' that the Medium tunes into.

I think it may be worthwhile here to clarify the difference between a spirit and a ghost. A spirit is an element of our eternal selves that resides in a different dimension to our own. They are able to interact with us through mediums or through their ability to visit us in dream visitations or they may be able to manipulate and exert an influence over objects in our dimension. Frequently after a loved one has passed to spirit, the grieving relatives will report many strange instances of electronic apparatus mysteriously turning itself on and off at random. I can vouch for this as when a very close relative of mine died, every time we mentioned his name the doorbell would ring. There was never anyone at the door when we checked, and the other amazing thing was that instead of the usual ding-dong noise that the bell made, when my relative was manipulating it, it only ever made the ding sound. This became such a common occurrence that it went way beyond the chances of it being coincidence, and as daft as it sounds, it also served to offer an enormous amount of comfort and laughter, which I suppose was the intention. He didn't stop at doorbells though; on one occasion his daughter arose early one morning and prepared herself for work. She turned on the TV and hopped into the shower. Ten minutes later she re-entered the bedroom only to find that the TV had mysteriously changed channels by itself. It was now showing the video of her late fathers favourite song, 'World on a String' by Michael Buble. The intention once again was obviously to offer some comfort. Ghosts on the other hand, don't seem to have any ability to interact with us. I think of them in the same way as if watching a film at the cinema, whereby an image is projected onto a screen, and although we can see it we cannot influence it or have it influence us; we simply don't appear in their world. They are just snapshots of instances from another time. This is why ghosts are said to be able to walk through walls, because in their time the wall wasn't there. What we are seeing is a video playback of an occurrence in space and time. There is one instance of an apparition of a group of soldiers marching through a cellar who were only visible from the waist up. This is because they were marching along the old roadway, which lay two feet below the modern day floor.

It is important to remember that these TV shows fall into the category of light entertainment and we shouldn't place too much emphasis on them as serious scientific experiments. I have seen plenty of episodes where they do seem to have caught examples of genuine paranormal behaviour, but I am sure there must be times when nothing in particular seems to be happening that somebody may be tempted to offer a 'helping hand'. Any kind of small object could be secreted about the person and be bought out to play at the appropriate moment and would almost certainly guarantee the perpetrator an appearance in the final edit.

I could stake a claim to have invented the paranormal investigation genre. My first foray into this field was as an eleven year old, when my best friend Helen, and I, did our first ghost hunt. The haunted house in question lay a mile down a deserted farm track on a lonely and neglected footpath on the way to a village called... 'Wychnor' *My god! What more evidence do you need?* We had passed it frequently on the way to her Grandfather's house. The cottage was a tumbling mass of porous bricks and overgrown brambles and was every inch the archetypel haunted house, all that was missing was a belfry with bats flying around it. Opposite, on the other side of the muddy track was a spinney of trees, in amongst which was a large marshy bog, known locally as 'death-pond.' and many's the time we sprinted past it with the devil snapping at our heels. We took a solemn vow to explore it fully during the forthcoming summer holidays.

Helen shared my passion for all things mystical and was as keen as me to find out about the afterlife. Even at age 11, we were old hands at Parapsychology. We didn't call it by that title of course; to us it was just *weird stuff*. There was a time when we were convinced that the Spirit World was trying to contact us through my tape-recorder. I had a cassette of the *Beatles*, and half way through 'Let It Be' the tape went funny and the sound faded in and out, as if *Paul McCartney* was singing backwards through a bucket. We played and then re-wound the strange noise numerous times trying desperately to decipher this message from the *great beyond*. Someone, or something, was definitely trying to make contact. After hours of listening intently we finally de-coded the veiled astral message. It was:

'HADOCK, HADOCK, BELLYFLOP, POODLE!'

So you can see – we had nothing to fear from a silly old haunted house. That summer saw us packing a rucksack with all the ghost hunting tools we thought we would need; an old torch minus batteries, some green garden twine, two bags of sweets and a broken penknife stolen from my dad's shed; who needs night vision camera's anyway?

We returned to the cottage in the woods and found it boarded-up and near derelict. Since our last visit the brambles had tightened their grip on the property and appeared to be digesting the building brick-by-brick. We managed to fight our way to the back door. The paint had peeled away to reveal bleached wood like old bones on a half rotten carcass. Being chivalrous and having been taught *ladies first*, I gallantly let Helen open the door. I stood six paces back, in case I needed to make a run for it; to fetch help you understand. The door made the requisite creak for a haunted house, the same sound my Grandads back made when he stood up. Once inside, it took a moment for our eyes to become accustomed to the darkness. Shards of light, shone into the room through the boarded over windows. It was a small room with an earthen floor, an old sink balanced on some bricks, and a broken table; from the beams hung a lone saucepan, red-through with rust. The smell was a mixture of dust and damp; a sickly-sweet fug that you could taste at the back of your throat. Inside was complete silence, the noises from outside unable to penetrate this otherworldly place. I thought a few comforting words might be in order, "It's as quiet as a grave," I said, "perhaps we should come back another time... there might be a dead body sat upright in a rocking-chair in the next room." After all, I didn't want Helen to be frightened. "Come on, you big puff," she said striding towards the next closed door. "Let's take a proper look around." I followed at a discreet distance. The door to the main room hung limply from one hinge, looking like a broken tooth. As it was pushed open the bottom of the door caught on the floor and sent a stream of dust up into the air. The particles hung heavily in the atmosphere and the foggy cloud was caught in the shadowy light from the windows, looking for all the world as if a Spectre would materialize out of it at any second. This next room was again bare, except for an old iron range cut into one wall; a bird's nest blocking the grate. Lumps of plaster lay shattered over the floor leaving gaping scars in the wall surface. I'd seen enough and was ready to leave, but Helen suggested we see what was upstairs. I glanced across to the skeletal staircase in the corner. The second and forth steps were missing and the others looked none to safe. "It's probably best if you go first," I kindly suggested, "the stairs don't look as if they will support the weight of two." She scaled them easily and stood at the top staring back at me with a questioning look. The upper room was pretty much like the rest of the house, only a little brighter as the grimy upper window had not been boarded up. The ceiling had collapsed in one corner, revealing the roof space. Daylight shone through the gaps in the tiles, like stars in the night sky. Fingers of ivy had crept under the eaves and secured themselves in a stranglehold around old brickwork. The wooden floor creaked like a galleon as we walked around on it, sagging dangerously under our combined weight. Luckily, neither of us were chubby kids and had only lunched on *black-jacks* and *fruit-salads* on the journey there. I still had a packet of *tooti-frooties*, but I was saving those for the long walk home. If we ever made it out alive that is.

Helen was opening a cupboard door when we heard voices, 'oh god', I thought to myself, 'it's a coven of witches coming to get us.' Helen had moved to the window,

"Hey, look whose coming." she said excitedly. I ran over and looked down to the muddy track. Two girls were walking towards the old property, talking loudly together. I recognised them as being from the same road as us in the village. "Hey, that's Rhoda Slapton and Thelma Pitts," I said, "I bet they're not brave enough to come in here..."

Of course, I was wrong. As a kid, if a signs says 'Wet Paint,' what do you do? You touch it of course, and, like moths drawn to a flame, the two girls decided the chance to explore a *haunted* house was too good to miss. "Quick!" Helen whispered, "Into the cupboard." We pulled open the double doors of the floor-to-ceiling closet and squeezed inside, closing the doors behind us, leaving a tiny crack to peer through. We could hear the snap of broken twigs under foot as the girls made their way through the protective thicket of brambles and scrub, towards the back door. Being trapped in a dark confined space made my heart leap about violently and I could hear it thumping wildly in my ears. No two-ways about it – I was scared.

However, I wasn't as terrified as the two girls who now pushed open the back door. We could hear their muffled voices, nervous and fearful. "Hellooo..." came a weak cry, as they shuffled into the downstairs room. "Oh God, it's horrible!" There was the odd gasp, as one of them spotted an enormous spider's web. "It smells of wee," said the other. The sound of their feet scraping on the dusty earthen floor echoed around the empty rooms. A door groaned open with the sound of a coffin lid being lifted, and the girls made their way into the main room.

"Don't let go of my hand." One of them cautioned. We could tell from the clarity of their voices that they had reached the bottom of the stairs. As one of them trod on the first step, it splintered and snapped beneath her feet, both girls screamed. "Walk at the edge, not the middle." One quietly warned. As they slowly and carefully made their way up the broken stairs, we gradually saw the top of their heads come into view from our secret vantage point. In slow motion, they crept further up towards us, and as they were nearing the top they paused and looked hesitantly around, their heads turning nervously left and right, scanning for danger.

Helen nudged me. She held up her fingers and mouthed the words, "After three..." and then made a silent screaming face. The girls took one more step and I looked to Helen. She lowered each finger in turn, three...two...one...we punched open the doors and exploded out with the most terrifying howl, hands clawing at thin air and teeth bared, wailing like two beasts from the bowels of hell. Our screams were drowned out by those of the two poor girls. I don't think they even saw us. Their eyes, although wide open, were blinded by fear. I'd never really heard a cry of utter terror before. Sheer panic set in and they turned-tail and leapt down the stairs. Still screaming, they burst through the house, the back door was thrown open with manic force in their desperate bid to escape. They continued shrieking as they ran wildly through the brambles, which snatched meanly at their bare legs. As they hit the footpath they came back into our view. They sprinted, hand-in-hand, as if being chased by an axe-murderer. They didn't look back. They ran and ran until they were lost from sight. We could still hear them screaming for a long while afterwards, until eventually their shrill cries were lost on the wind.

We both stood staring out of the window for a time, almost in a state of shock. I don't think either of us had fully comprehended how scared they would be. My guilt-ridden mind searched wretchedly for some redemption. I looked to Helen for some reassurance, a comforting word. "Got any fruit salads left?" She asked, "I'm starving!"

As you can see, I wasn't the bravest of young men. Helen met the world head on, ready to face anything. I could always be seen three paces back and peering timidly over her shoulder, but unlike me, she hadn't grown up under the threat and 'all seeing eye' of the evil paranormal entity that was Mr Cactypusscat.

He was a half-man, half-wolf creature that was my family's version of the Bogey Man, who for some unexplained reason lived behind the gas fire in our lounge. I never quite worked out how a six-foot half-breed managed to get in and out from behind the fire, but as my sister was always telling me, "He's magic and obeys my every command."

I was led to believe that my mortal soul was in peril, and the threat of Mr. Cactypusscat was used to bribe me for years. The risk of a visit from him was enough to persuade me to do any manner of laborious tasks. "Nick, if you don't tidy my bedroom Mr Cactypusscat is going to eat your face in the night!" Or "Nick, if you tell on me, Mr. Cactypusscat is going to bury you face-down under the rockery." I was scared witless by these taunts.

One day I called her bluff and said I didn't believe in him. A look of determination crossed her face. She frowned at me, pushing her eyebrows together so that they formed a single hairy bridge over her eyes. With hands on hips she shouted, "Oh Mr. Cactypusscat, your presence is requested!" She began to stamp her feet up and down in turn, "One...Two...Three... I can hear him waking up." She said. By the time she reached seven I could imagine Mr. Cactypusscat sliding his vile head out from under the gas fire, his nose twitching as he sniffed for fresh blood, his long tongue sliding over his fangs in an attempt to catch the frothy saliva that was forming on them. "Ok, ok, you win!" I would shout hysterically, tears burning the back of my eyes. "We can play *'lets pretend we're Peter's and Lee'* but I want to wear the sunglasses this time."

My parents occasionaly used Mr. Cactypusscat as a threat against me, but they also knew of other ways to induce me to do their bidding, "Nick," my dad would urge, "nip to the shop son, and get me 10 embassy-tipped and a *Sports Argos*, you can get yourself a sherbet-dip out of the change." There wasn't much that could drag me away from *The Basil Brush Show*, but the promise of a sherbet-dip would have me slipping on my trainers and disappearing out the door in a flash. I'd dash through the estate at break-neck speed, passing my mates playing football in the street,

"Nick," they'd holler after me, "fancy a game?"

"Can't stop," I'd call over my shoulder, "Sherbet-Dip!" They understood; this bizarre sweet held a strange fascination for us. Shaped like a stick of dynamite, it contained powdered sherbet and had a stick of black liquorice poking through the top. The idea was to suck the sherbet through the liquorice stick, but the sherbet was impossible to reach as you got towards the end of the tube, so you ended up ripping open the end of the packet and lifting the tube to your mouth. Most of the powder would tip out over your face leaving you with a sherbet moustache, giving the appearance of a heavy cocaine user. The next problem was extricating the cardboard from your wet lips, having sucked out all the moisture, the card would be glued to your face and would require the help of two friends to remove it, usually along with three layers of skin.

By the time I returned home I'd be frothing at the mouth and panting like a rabid dog. I'd present my dad with his beloved cigarettes and newspaper, whereupon he would head straight for the bathroom, the door would be bolted and he would be lost to the world for hours on end. The only signs of occupation were spirals of blue smoke creeping from under the door and the strains of a Carpenters song being sung, however it was never done perfectly – the tune might be correct but the lyrics would always be wrong,

"Stop, oh yeah, wait a minute Mr. Milkman. *Ple e e ease* – Mr Milkman. Please Mr. Milkman look and see, if there's a pinta in your sack for me..."

He would emerge, hours later smelling of fags, looking tired and drawn and complaining of pins-and-needles in his feet. I believe Mr Cactypusscat was another handy tip my father had picked up in Parenting School under the section 'Bogey Men and Their Uses as Tools for Bribery in the Family Environment.'

Strangely, for someone normally so non-committal about life after death or the existence of ghosts, it is my dad who has the most profound experiences of all. For instance, he saw the spirit of his own dad shortly after he had died. He was awoken during the night to see his own father walking through a wall towards him. Unsure what to make of the situation he said,

"Hello."

"Hello son," replied Granddad, "I'm just making sure you're all right."

"Yeah, I'm fine. Anyway, you're the one who's dead, how are you?" my dad responded.

"Not so bad thanks..."

They then spent ten minutes staring at each other in complete silence, feeling awkward and unsure what to say.

But then they didn't chat much when Granddad was alive, so why should things be any different between them now he had passed to spirit?

How do you chat with a spirit anyway? What do you have in common with them now that they are free of their physical body?

'See the match on Saturday?'

'No I'm dead!'

'Oh yeah, sorry. What you driving now?'

'Don't drive anymore – I'm dead.'

'Oh right. What's the food like over there?'

'I don't eat, I no longer have a stomach – I'm dead.'

'Damn, sorry, forgot. Got any plans for the weekend?'

'Um, still dead...'

So, did my father make up this encounter? Or was this meeting some figment of his imagination? I find it hard to believe that he would invent a scenario that was the complete antithesis to all his belief systems. Why imagine a situation he didn't believe was possible? I find it perfectly feasible that the 'soul energy' of my grandfather found a way to bridge the gap between two worlds so that he could come and visit his son. After all, he wasn't just his body when he was alive. There was a man inside of that body, thinking, rationalising and observing the world around him.

Why shouldn't that 'conscious energy' part of my grandfather carry on after his body had given up?

I've tried Mr Cactypusscat on my own kids, but to no avail. No matter how hard I try to 'come the heavy' with them, I always come across as wholly unconvincing and they just laugh at me. They watch things on TV that, thirty years ago, would have required an 18 certificate, and that's only on the children's channel. Somewhere along the line, childhood has lost its innocence and I can't help feeling that children are exposed to so much more menace via TV and video games these days that they are almost immune to it. They have been robbed of some of the wonders of childhood.

When I was young I was so gullible that I took every word an adult said to me as the gospel truth. I was scared of everything; Very occasionally I still see flashes of innocence in my own kids, and it's wonderful to behold. One such occasion was a few years ago when my youngest son Jim, then aged 5, decided to dress up for Halloween. We had bought him a red-devil mask, complete with horns, which he took great delight in wearing constantly, (including in his bed whilst asleep.) Unfortunately, within days he had lost it, and so when his big moment came to go' trick or treating' he had to make do with another mask that was a memento of a recent party. Our puzzled neighbours found themselves opening their doors to be met with the sight of a little boy giving muffled roars from behind a bright yellow Giraffe mask. To give them their due, they did put on a good show of pretending to be scared witless. He was well satisfied.

Now call it synchronicity or coincidence but whilst I was working on this chapter a very strange thing happened. It started with a phone call;

"Guess what your dad's just seen in the back garden?" It was my mother and she sounded a bit more excited than was good for her. This is one of those daft questions that mum's come up with every now and again. Others include, 'Guess who I saw last week?' 'Guess what I've just bought?' and the ever-popular 'Guess who's died?'

"Is it an elephant?" A stab in the dark but worth a try I thought.

"A ghost!" she said.

Damn it! I couldn't believe I'd guessed wrong again. I swallowed my disappointment and impeached her to put my dad on the phone.

"Well, I was just painting the landing," he said, "When I happened to look out of the window and noticed someone walking across the lawn. It struck me as strange because nobody can get into the garden without coming through the house. I knew your mother was downstairs so it couldn't have been her so I took a closer look. It was a tall lady dressed in what looked like a nun's robes. She was all in white and walked slightly hunched over and reminded me of the kind of person you would see in a medieval painting. She walked slowly across the lawn and then went through the wall into the neighbour's garden. I remember thinking to myself that that's a ghost, and yet I don't believe in them. It was really strange but I didn't find it scary." Once again it would seem that the non-believer was the one to have the paranormal experience. (And I haven't even mentioned the time he spent twenty minutes watching a UFO, which he can still describe it in minute detail!)

A couple of days later I noticed something unusual in my own back garden. I could see something large and black in the middle of the lawn. On closer investigation it proved to be a dead rook. Its blue-black feathers looked pristine and had a satin sheen to them. The beautiful bird looked in perfect condition and showed no signs of having been attacked; in fact there wasn't a mark on it. It was just lying serenely on its back with its little legs sticking up in the air. What was unusual was that its wings were folded neatly behind it. If it had fallen out of a tree or been fighting for its life the wings would surely have been outstretched or have showed some visible signs of a struggle. Its perfect heart shaped outline and serene countenance made it look for all the world like a tiny black Angel that had been delicately placed on the ground. I have to admit it left me slightly puzzled.

Later that evening my father rang me with the shocking news that his younger sister had sadly died that same day.

***

Peggy came into my life about three years ago. I don't remember how; she suddenly appeared one day at work and we hit it off instantly. She is a lively 84 year-old with a shock of silver-grey hair. She suffers terribly with arthritis and a serious heart condition, but you never hear her complain. Quite often I'll be working away, head down, engrossed over the inner workings of someone's precious timepiece, when I get the feeling somebody is watching me. As I glance up Peggy's sunny smile will be shining back at me. One minute she's nowhere in sight, and then, 'PING', suddenly she's there, as if out of thin air. (A bit like the shopkeeper in Mr Benn) She waits patiently at the side of my counter and every week her requirement is the same: a cuddle. Nothing else, just a long hug is all that she desires, and who am I to deny an old lady a grope? I only charge her £5 a go! No... It's nice to know that time and dodgy joints haven't diminished her ability to grab my fleshy bits. It's a genuinely lovely feeling to hold her in my arms and feel her cold cheek against mine. She always smells of clean washing, lifebuoy soap and lily of the valley. I think it's important to let your guard down sometimes, to feel human; it's so easy to believe that we live in a sterile world, but we don't. I don't know anybody who doesn't like to be liked.

Mr Mick is another person who gives freely of himself. He's always happy, and this 96 year-old Irishman still rides his pushbike everywhere. Children adore him, his soft accent and big watery, Labrador eyes give him a gentle, unthreatening air. He's a great tonic and another person who has the ability to brighten your day with a funny story

He and his wife, also 96, recently had a short hotel break. As Mr Mick was signing in at reception, his wife made her way to the elevator. As she waited for the lift doors to open, she turned around and shouted across the crowded foyer,

"Michael, did you remember to pack the condoms?"

"Gotta suitcase full of them me darlin'," he shouted back.

He's also the person who taught me a valuable lesson in keeping a sense of perspective. I was having a particularly trying day. Nothing seemed to be going right

"What's the matter with you?" he asked. "You're not your usual sunny self today."

"Oh just a bit stressed Mick," I said in a self-pitying tone.

"Stress, you say? Stress..? What is it nowadays with everybody bein' obsessed wi' stress? Dats all you hear about. Stress 'cause I can't afford dis, and stress 'cause I want dat, and can't have it. Let me tell you about stress. When I was your age, I had 40 thousand Germans tryin' to shoot me up the arse. Now that's stress!"

Chapter 4
HI SPIRITS!

"Can you hear me mother?"
Sandy Powell

Whatever happened to ectoplasm? It's the spiritual equivalent of fuzzy-felt - you never hear of it anymore. There was a time when any medium worth their salt would fill the room with this strange candyfloss-type substance. In the case of one famous medium, it would stream out of their mouth into the shape of the spirit attempting to communicate, where upon it would converse with the gathering. Imagine that - talking candyfloss – fantastic! You never won that at any fairground I ever visited. I did once win a goldfish in a polythene bag, but that was by mistake. I was trying to win a *Mark Strong* doll. He was a sort of bargain basement version of *Action-Man*, without the real hair or gripping hands, although when you pressed a button in the middle of his back he did karate chop a bit of plastic plank in half. My ping-pong ball had landed in the wrong jam-jar, and instead of a 6 inch killing machine with interchangeable tracksuits, I ended up with a mangy fish in a bag – so, no *Mark Strong* and no candyfloss – talking or otherwise.

I think ectoplasm belongs to a by-gone era of medium-ship. Back then you had to be called Doris to stand *any* chance of getting on a stage - even if you were a man. Yesterday's mediums looked like your Aunty Phyllis. They wore big flowery dresses and support tights, had whiskers on their chins, and drank milk stout. They were the kind of women who knew how to make gravy and there was an honest integrity about them. They seemed safe and reliable. They didn't go in for today's showbiz antics. They could probably do a nationwide tour with two nylon dresses from C&A and a pair of stout shoes. So long as they had access to a purple rinse 24 hours a day, they were happy.

I first became interested in mediums by reading the wonderful books by *Doris Stokes,* but it was many years until I had my first private sitting. Scouring the local paper one evening, Dilly and I saw an advert for a lady offering private clairvoyant readings from her home. She had studied at the London psychic college, an establishment set up to test, help, and further-improve the technique of anybody with mediumistic ability. We knew their testing was rigorous, and this clinched our decision to book.

On the evening in question the lady agreed to see us both at the same time. She asked only for our first names and suggested that we take a cassette tape to record the sitting. We were both looking forward to the experience, but were a little nervous. We need not have worried as the lady was most welcoming. The front door opened, and as her head peaked around the corner, her face lit up as if we were some long-lost relatives dropping by unexpectedly.

"I'm Mrs. Plum." she said opening the door wide. She was a small lady, probably late middle-aged, with a trace of a Scottish accent. As we entered her hallway there came the sound of distant thunder; within seconds' dozens of dogs appeared from every doorway. They fell over each other in their enthusiasm to reach us and have the honour of licking and slobbering all over us. Mrs. Plum stood amongst the wagging tails and flapping ears, just managing to keep her balance, she smiled down at the mass of fur, as if looking at naughty children.

"No black cats in this house, as you can see," she laughed. The noise was incredible, yapping, yelping, barking, panting, and I think I detected the odd trump. An old grey Labrador skulked away looking guilty. Mrs. Plum sniffed, "Oh, what a way to welcome guests," she said, "Right my dears, make your way upstairs, second door on the left."

Once upstairs, we entered a nicely furnished low-lit room. Mrs. Plum followed us and closed the door, blocking out the noise from downstairs. She sat down opposite me and explained what we were to expect. Settling back into her chair, she lit up a cigarette. I glanced at the ashtray, from the look of it - this wasn't her first of the day. She visibly relaxed, closed her eyes and remained silent for around five minutes. Any minute now she's going to start snoring, I thought, but no...

"Who's Tony?" she asked. My chin hit the floor. Dilly gave a great gasp and grabbed my arm. How on earth did she know my father's name? I'd never met this woman before. There was no way she could have sensed anything from my body language, and she didn't even 'try out' a few names first. This was straight in with outstanding evidence. "I've got your dad's father with me," she confided. She then went on to explain what he'd done for a living and gave other information and personal details. I was absolutely thrilled, dumbstruck, happy – any number of emotions rolled into one.

Next it was the turn of my wife's jaw to drop. "I have your grandmother with me and she's talking about Margaret." she said. Dilly explained that Margaret was her mother's name. Once again, no other erroneous names had been offered. "She's saying Margaret takes too much upon herself, she needs to slow down a bit, but she's the kind of woman who will just laugh and say, 'yes, yes, alright then, so who's going to make me a nice cup of tea?' Mrs. Plum went on to describe my mother-in-law perfectly. She then remarked that Grandma was talking about a disagreement over a ring in the family, but my wife had no knowledge of this. "Ask your mum about it when you see her." she suggested. After 40 minutes, and as many cigarettes, the reading was over. We both left feeling absolutely astounded, and smelling of fags.

It's interesting to note that soon afterwards we played the tape of our conversation to our respective parents. My father's reaction was a joy. He is a committed and fully paid up member of *Sceptics Anonymous,* ' When you're dead, you're dead!' is the nearest he comes to uttering a judgment on the afterlife.

"And who's Tony?" the voice on the tape asked. At that moment he was so shocked his eyebrows shot up over his forehead and hit the wall behind him. "How in heaven did she know my name...?" he yelped, his voice going up three octaves – like an audition for the *Bee Gees.* Open mouthed, he stared at me, then at Dilly, then finally at my mother, and then back and forth between the three of us. The expression on his face was such that we all fell about laughing. "How, what, why…" he was starting to stammer. "D-D-Did you tell her my name?" We assured him that of course we hadn't. We played him the rest of the tape, at the end of which he said, "Well, I don't know what to make of that, I don't know what I believe anymore. I'll have to go to bed to think about it." With that he got up and walked out of the room, only to reappear ten minutes later in his vest and pants. "However did she know all that?" he asked again. He really was flummoxed.

My mother-in-law's reaction was equally entertaining. We played the tape up until the point where the medium says "She's saying she takes too much upon herself, she needs to slow down a bit... " We pressed pause. My mother-in-law gave a wry laugh. "Yes, yes, alright then, so who's going to make me a nice cup of tea?" she inquired. We re-started the tape; she had said the *exact* comments the medium had uttered, not one word different.

"Oh my good god!" was her reaction. "Play that again." We did so, and she still could not quite believe it. Her baffled look amused my father-in-law greatly; he didn't get many opportunities to make fun of his more forceful wife. He started to laugh at her predicament, but was soon subdued with her next choice of words, "You can pack that in matey," she said, "Or *you'll* be talking to spirit sooner than you intended!" . When the tape came to the part about *the ring*, my mother-in-law revealed that years before, there had been a family feud over who inherited the grandmother's wedding ring. My wife had never heard this story until her own grandmother had passed it on through Mrs. Plum.

Although Mrs. Plum was my first *private* sitting, I had seen mediums before. I had attended a Spiritualist Church meeting with some family friends. The church was an old Victorian building tucked away along a backstreet of my local town. The meeting itself was a bit like a school assembly, only here there was no prizes for needlework, no soggy-dogs flicked onto the back of your neck, and no Adam Bunting farting loudly on the wooden chairs. Out of force of habit I felt I should stand in the corner and face the wall. Instead, I went and found a seat.

The room had that smell of old buildings, a fusty, damp aroma and the faint whiff of clammy stockings, although that might have been emanating from the old dear sat next to me. She looked the kind of lady who knew her way around a pair of zip-up boots and a pull-along shopping trolley. "Do you fancy a hotty?" she asked. As chat-up lines go, I thought this a strange one, but then I noticed she was holding a crumpled paper bag towards me full of Victory V lozenges. I declined this thoughtful invitation. My grandfather always kept a packet of these firebrand sweets in his pocket. They could strip the enamel from your teeth in seconds and make your eyes water more than crushing your privates on the crossbar of your Raleigh Olympus 5 speed. Every Saturday afternoon I would settle down with him to watch the wrestling on TV and out would come the lozenges. Every week I tried one and each time it nearly killed me. Was this offer from the lady a sign that perhaps my granddad was still around? I looked at her again, a little bit closer this time. Hmmm... she did have similar teeth to Granddad, and excessive earwax as well. She must have caught me staring because she turned, smiled and the bag was offered once more. She was obviously an old hand at spiritualism because when they announced who the medium was for the evening, she closed her eyes and nodded approvingly. She leaned over and whispered in my ear that they were the best in the area.

After a few prayers and hymns, the lady medium strode on stage in a no-nonsense kind of manner. She was a large middle-aged woman with a friendly face, ample bosom and hairy legs. If there was a fight, I'd want her on my side. She gave a few messages around the packed hall and then pointed to my friend's mother. She had lost her husband a few months before and had decided to tag along with us at the last minute.

"This is a strange message my love," stated the medium, "It's a gentleman, but he won't tell me his name. Instead he says I am to repeat something from him." She stopped for a moment with a puzzled look on her face as if she couldn't quite understand what was being conveyed to her. "Okay, I'll tell her," she said looking to the heavens,

"I come to guide you from the valley of the shadow of death to the halls of glory. You have undergone trials and tribulations, yet be of good cheer. Charity will support you when tempted to lose heart, hope will cheer you on your path, and faith will comfort you in your darkest hour, shining like a beacon of truth into all the dark corners of your life, it will be your illumination"

This kind of rhetoric continued for a few more minutes. Everyone, including the medium, was looking mystified. Everyone that is, except for the recipient of the message. My friend's mother enlightened us.

"That's Masonic ritual; I used to help my husband learn it. That secret passage was part of the piece he learning before he passed."

***

One of the finest stage mediums I have seen was Bill Harrison. It was more like stand-up comedy than clairvoyance, as Bill never missed the chance for a laugh, at his or the audience's expense. Obviously, some people are attending under traumatic circumstances, but Bill seemed able to give readings and information in such a happy and positive manner that even those people who were grieving found themselves laughing and crying at the same time. His demonstrations were always upbeat affairs, and I'm sure one of the reasons he was so accurate was down to all the laughter he created. With a high vibration in the room, perhaps it is easier for spirit to make a connection. I remember him giving Dilly a message once.

"I've got a man in spirit for you. He's not very tall and he tells me he's an uncle on your father's side. He's showing me rolling hills so I think he lived in the countryside. He says you will know who he is because he's got his trouser leg rolled up and he's giving me a funny handshake." Dilly laughed. There was only one person who fitted that description. Her Uncle Ernest had lived in the heart of the Cotswolds and been a life-long freemason. She wasn't unduly surprised that he should come through, as during his lifetime he had been a renowned faith healer and had a picture of his Native American spirit guide hanging proudly in his lounge for as long as Dilly could remember. Bill continued.

"Now he's looking serious and telling me about a friend of yours called Annabell. Does this make sense?" he asked. Dilly confirmed that she had a friend by that name.

"He is saying to watch out for her. She isn't the friend she purports to be and is a bit two faced." he started to laugh; "Actually, what he is showing me is this!" Bill then pretended to load an imaginary shotgun, raise it to his shoulder, take aim and fire it.

"Now don't get me wrong," he said with a cheeky grin, "He isn't telling you to go and shoot her, just to 'blow her off' as it were." This confirmed her suspicions about this friend. "He also says you have been doing some family history?" Dilly nodded, "I am being shown an old photograph of some Cavalry men dressed in khaki uniforms. I get the impression they may be in India or Africa, does this make sense?" Once again this was confirmed. Dilly is a keen genealogist, and only that week had been cataloguing some old family photos, one of which had been a faded picture of a great grandfather who had served in the Fifth Lancers during the Boer War. The picture was exactly as Bill had described it, even down to the amount of people featured in the photo." As we left the auditorium that evening, I remember being struck by how happy everybody looked. What a wonderful gift, I thought. Strangely, Bill passed over to spirit himself shortly after this. .

Without wishing to come across as a strange 'psychic groupie,' I have also closely followed the career of Gordon Smith, *AKA – The Psychic Barber ("Short, back and sides' sir? Oh, and by the way, your Aunty Ethel is telling me she knows it was you who poisoned her cat.")* And of all the mediums I have seen, Gordon is without doubt the best. (I would expect nothing less from the seventh son of a seventh son.) His accuracy is truly astonishing, and what I really like about him is his integrity, humility and his respect for those in the spirit world. He never charges for a private sitting and I have always felt that he gives readings for the relief and comfort that it can bring to a grieving loved one. As he says in his book *The Unbelievable Truth,* "Working with spirit reminds me how many people need contact with their loved ones. Sometimes just a little word from heaven can change so much how they are feeling."

Gordon's remarkable gift was first apparent when he was a young child. He would frequently see deceased friends and neighbours. This never seemed to bother him, but those around him felt uncomfortable with it and so he 'shut down'. It wasn't until he reached his early twenties that it really made itself apparent again. One night he was awoken to discover the brother of a good friend standing at the bottom of his bed wanting to talk. The next day Gordon discovered that this young man had died that very night in a fire. By this time Gordon was earning his living as a barber, (I've heard of *Voices from beyond the grave,* could these be termed *Snippets from beyond the fringe?)* and I can't help but wonder how many people must have come in hoping for a reading rather than a rinsing. He then started to attend a spiritualist church, and with the help of a development circle, his talents could be properly directed.

Gordon has had extensive testing of his abilities by Professor Archie Roy of Glasgow University, with blind, double blind and even triple blind testing all coming out with results in his favour. I asked him about this once at a book signing, and wondered if it ever bothered him that people were always asking him to prove his abilities. He said that it wasn't his job to prove to people that we live on after we die, and that to some people no proof is enough anyway. His job was to bring comfort and healing to people in need of it. He now travels the world doing just that.

As you can see I have seen many mediums, and overall my experiences have all been positive. However, in the interest of fairness and impartiality I must say that not all of them were up to scratch. There were those who were perhaps just having an 'off' night, there were others whose intentions were better than their abilities, and then there were those who were just out for an ego trip.

I saw a particularly poor one recently. She came onto the stage wearing a costume that wouldn't have looked out of place in *Lord of the Rings;* she wore a huge amulet around her neck and had more rings on her fingers than Mr T.

"C'mon everybody," she bellowed. "Get with it!"

She then proceeded to play loud rock music in a bid to get the crowd going. At this point the only place I felt like going was out the door.

"Clap your hands," she ordered, striding up the isles. Any minute now, I thought, she'll start playing the air-guitar. The group of pensioners in the front-row looked rather bemused. It wasn't long before she picked on one of these elderly folk and said,"I'm getting a song from spirit for you, it's called *Daisy Daisy,*" she sang three bars of the song, "Now I don't know this song," she continued, "I've never heard it before…"

Never heard it before? What rot! She was a middle-aged woman; I have a seven-year-old niece who can give you three verses of *Daisy Daisy.*

Things went even further downhill when she approached a large man with a shaven head and long ponytail. He had a big bushy beard, a cut-off leather jacket and tattoos disappearing into every orifice. She closed her eyes, put her hands to her temples and gave a sigh like a punctured dinghy.

"I don't know why they're telling me this," she said, hamming it up "but do you have anything to do with motorbikes?" That's like asking a man in a dog-collar, 'Pardon me, but do you happen do be religious?'

To my great delight the man said "No". She looked stunned.

"Oh, right," she was getting flustered, "Well, perhaps it's because someone you know will be buying one soon." She walked away rather quickly. Her eyes machine-gunned the room, looking for another victim. She picked on a teenage girl and fired four or five names at her in quick succession, which all missed the target. She tutted, put her hands on her hips and raised her eyes to the heavens. "Come on you lot up there, you're not very good tonight," she said, shifting the blame, "You know it can be quite a burden sometimes, having this gift." Nobody looked very sympathetic.

It must be great to be a genuine medium. You'd never lose or misplace anything again; a quick chat with 'them upstairs' and the answer's yours in an echoing voice *"Your missing sock is down the back of the sofa."* or *"Quick, Mrs. Penberthy is coming down your path, pretend you are out!"* or even *"Don't forget, Top Gear is on at 8 o'clock tonight."* Of course there is probably a downside. Being woken at 3 o'clock in the morning by a dead person pulling on your toes and wanting a chat might be a little inconvenient.

Unfortunately, I don't appear to have any clairvoyant or psychic capabilities. The nearest I get to predicting the future is when agreeing to a second helping of prawn-bhuna and saying, "Cor, I'm gonna regret this in the morning!" However, I have *pretended* to be clairvoyant many times. One of my favourite tricks is to quickly glance into customers' wallets as they pay, searching for clues as to their identity. Old ladies are always good because their bus pass is nearly always on show. When handing them their change I say,

"Thanks Dorothy, that's £3 change." For a moment, they are silent and just look at you, obviously wondering why they don't recognize you.

"How do you know my name?" they ask.

"It is Dorothy isn't it? Dorothy Collins?"

"Well yes, but how…?"

"Oh, it's just the spirits talking in my head." I say. I then work my way through the most bizarre story I can come up with. "It's just one of your cousins warning me to be careful of you, because you're quite partial to young men, and it has been known for you to entice them back to your warden-controlled apartment and hold them prisoner for weeks on end, making them vacuum in the nude whilst listening to Glen Miller',s *'In the Mood'* and only feeding them Kit-e-Kat." Obviously such ridiculous stories are never believed and they start to laugh.

"Come on," they say, "have we met before?" I then come clean about seeing their name on show in their purses. "You cheeky young bugger," is the standard reply. I have to be careful though to make sure I pick on a good sport. It does show, however, how easy it would be to con someone if you were of that ilk, or not, as the case may be.

One day I spotted a girl whom I recognized from my school days. It had been the best part of 25 years since I'd seen her, but she had a very distinctive look about her that I remembered. She was looking at an item to purchase so I walked over to help,

"Can I be of assistance, Gail?" I asked. Her head shot around towards me.

"Uh, what..? Who are you?" she barked. Seeing her close up, I knew I wasn't mistaken. I closed my eyes, starting to ham it up.

"Don't worry my sweetheart, it,s just spirit talking to me. Yes, the name is Gail - now wait and see if I can get the second name." Here I paused and took a few deep breaths. "Yes, it's coming, it's Daw, Dawkins... no, no, it's DAWSON!" I bellowed triumphantly. She looked shocked. I didn't stop there; I went on to tell her the village she had lived in, the school she had attended and even that she had an older brother who had crashed his moped into the local phone box in 1979. All this was done with dramatic effect. She didn't say a word, just stood there open mouthed. I thought perhaps I'd better come clean.

"It's me Nick, Nick Richardson." I revealed. "Remember? We were in the same class at school." Here we go, I thought, this is where she screams as she recognizes me.

"Who..?" she asked, her eyes registering no one home. Her blank expression made me edgy. I was starting to lose my nerve.

"Nick Richardson?" I said, almost apologetically. I gave a wan smile. "John Russell Junior School, Miss Pitt's class; Miss Pitt hit me over the head with the dinner money tin for having the worst writing in class." Surely *now* she'd remember. I've certainly never forgotten - I still have the bruise. I keep it in a box under the bed. At this point I was starting to gabble. She looked me hard in the face.

"I have never laid eyes on you in my life before," she stated emphatically. She slammed the item she was holding back onto the shelf, turned and strode away with heavy footsteps. "Weirdo!" she spat over her shoulder. I looked around – everyone was staring. I quickly excused myself to the toilet inorder to wipe the egg from my face.

***

Choosing a medium you feel happy with for a private sitting can sometimes be tricky. You should never feel frightened or troubled; and they should only give you information that feels helpful. Mediums do not tell fortunes; if you want to look into your future, you need to go and see a psychic. Someone calling themselves a medium should be able to give you proof of the survival of life after death. However, it's what's real and true to you that counts. This is why the proof sometimes comes in the most ambiguous forms.

One of the craziest messages I ever received came from a medium during a crowded stage demonstration. He strode purposefully down the aisle, pointing at me.

"TOFFO'S!" he roared.

"I beg your pardon?"

"Toffo's," he repeated with a smile on his face. "But not the ordinary ones, these are the assorted flavoured ones that you loved. Your granny's just told me." He was correct. Every Saturday when I was young, my granny would visit and bring a huge bag of sweets, and first out of the bag and into my mouth would be the assorted flavoured toffo's. Especially the banana flavour; I'd kill for them. It's bizarre evidence like this that proves to me that our consciousness is eternal. If this man had been fishing for clues, it's most unlikely that he would have shouted such an obscure statement at me. It could have been an embarrassing moment though. I mean, what if he'd have asked to see my curly-wurly, or even worse, claim that I was partial to a suck on a fisherman's friend?

A good medium can provide incontrovertible proof of life after death. An accomplished clairvoyant doesn't even need to know your name before they can provide you with messages of enormous significance. Sceptics will often accuse mediums of 'cold reading'. This is where they supposedly pick-up sub-conscious signals from your body language or your reactions to certain statements. This may be so, but how could they possibly tell you your parents' names, or the names of your children? Quite often the evidence provided isn't earth shattering, but it *is* significant, and normally only something that you would know about. Often times you may not realise the implication until after the event. Perhaps later, when talking to a relative, new light is thrown onto a subject you thought didn't concern you, or the medium had got wrong. Let's face it, you can't glean the name of someone's dead husband from the way they cross their legs or raise their eyebrows.

Getting a recommendation from a satisfied friend is always a good way to find a medium. Taking a trip to your local spiritualist church is another, and it's always worth checking to see if a medium is affiliated with any recognized associations. It's important to remain open-minded during a reading. You may not make contact with the person you have in mind. You can't call on them to attend. They will only come if they can or want to.

***

So if all Jack Bell's stories were true, I had to get to the bottom of his Shirley MacLaine tale. The next time Jack visited; he took little persuasion to spill the beans.

After his retirement from live performing, he formed his own company selling musical instruments and travelled widely in Europe and the USA. It was in this capacity that he met Shirley MacLaine. She was performing her one-woman show in London; Jack was in town on business, and knew many of the musicians playing in her backing band. He telephoned one of them and managed to invite himself to the after show party. It was while he was talking to Ms MacLaine (no doubt putting her right on the finer points of acting technique) that she asked where he was staying in London. He told her that he hadn't yet booked a room anywhere. She told him she was staying in a hotel suite that had three bedrooms, and since she couldn't sleep in all of them and why didn't he take one? Jack's eyes lit up. Not at the thought of spending a night with a famous and beautiful actress, oh no, to Jack this was far more exciting, because this meant a 'free' room for the night.

"Ta love," he said, "I'd better ring me missus and tell her where I am."

"Oh no let me do it," she said with a hint of mischief, "It will be a laugh."

And so Jack's wife received a phone call from one of Hollywood's top actresses, saying that Jack would be spending the night with her, and would this be ok? Jack's wife was delighted, for a start it meant that Jack wouldn't be sleeping in his tatty caravan that he sometimes towed behind his car into London – he would frequently park it in hotel car parks and ask for a special reduction if he could sleep in it overnight. Secondly, it meant she could claim bragging rights over all her friends that, 'Jack had spent the night with Shirley MacLaine.' It was one of the few times I heard the words 'Jack' and 'Spent' in the same sentence. I am also relieved that everything was proper and above board between Jack and Ms MacLaine. Her books have had a profound influence on my life and have helped to formulate so much of my thinking. I have huge admiration for the honest and brave way that she has written about her own beliefs in life after death, metaphysics and reincarnation. I would hate to have had my illusions of the great lady shattered, as they are; they are only enhanced by her generosity to a stranger.

***

Chapter 5

OLD HABITS DIE HARD

Reality is merely an illusion, albeit a very
persistent one.

Albert Einstein

I've long harboured a secret desire to have been Robert the Bruce. I can imagine myself running through heather-filled glens with my sporran swinging freely in the breeze, leaping thistles in a single bound. I'd have a big ginger beard long enough to wrap around my neck on cold days like a scarf. After all, I have the legs for a kilt and the arms for a straightjacket. But could it be possible that I have lived before? Is my ability to polish off a bottle of whiskey a night perhaps a throwback to a former life in the Highlands? Was I once a member of the MacDonald clan and instrumental in the invention of the cheese-burger, or even better a McCartney; one of the most-feared close-harmony singing clan's north of the Trossachs?

For years I found the concept of reincarnation very hard to come-to-terms with. The fact that I will live on in some form after my physical death has never really been too hard an idea for me to grasp, but the thought that I may have lived many times before was something altogether different. I started to research the subject and read every book I could lay my hands on. The closer I looked at the subject, the more it seemed to make sense. Two thirds of the world's population has a belief in reincarnation, and once I had looked at it objectively I realized why should it not be a possibility to be born more than once?

The first time I heard of reincarnation was as a teenager when I watched a BBC documentary about it. Up until that point in my life, the most paranormal thing I'd ever seen on TV was the Yorkshire terrier on *That's Life* that said *'Sausages!'*

This particular documentary had a fascinating case of reincarnation that featured an Australian lady, who under hypnosis claimed she had lived in England in a former existence. During the regression her accent changed to one of a west-country dialect. It could be proven that this lady had spent her whole life in Australia. She gave her name and told a story of living in 18th century England. She portrayed her life in detail, describing the house she had lived in. Her family were farm labourers, living in a building alongside the main farmhouse. She relayed how the floor was made up of flagstones, with one in particula, having a distinctive pattern on it. The hypnotherapist handed her a pencil and paper and asked her to draw it. The information she had disclosed was so concise that it enabled the producers of the program to check all the facts. They proved so accurate that they managed to pinpoint the place of her former existence. They approached the current owner and he gave them permission to investigate the building further. After clearing the floor of year's worth of muck, they did indeed find a flagstone floor; and there in the centre was a flagstone with a unique pattern on it. They placed the lady's drawing next to it. It was a perfect match! The program left a deep impression on me and left me fascinated in the subject. What other explanation could there be? In my mind, the most plausible and convincing reason was that this lady had indeed lived before.

Years later, when Dilly and I moved house, a friend brought us a subscription to a spiritual magazine as a moving-in present. Amongst the advertisements was one for a set of 'past life regression' cassette tapes, to be used at home. We decided this was a comfortable and convenient way to start our investigation into our own past lives. On playing the tape, the first hurdle to overcome was amusement. The beginning of the tape covered 'controlled breathing exercises.' We followed the instructions carefully, but were soon puffing, panting and hyperventilating so loudly we sounded like two old Labradors after a run on a hot day. We couldn't help but find it comical and broke down into fits of uncontrollable laughter.

Our next effort was more fruitful. This time I managed to avoid laughing and found myself in a relaxed state of mind. The feeling was not unpleasant, I knew I wasn't asleep; I was deeply relaxed but in full control of all my senses. The tape metaphorically walked you through a door and into a past-life. In my mind I could see three doors in front of me; and I chose the middle one to walk through. The first thing I was aware of was my sandaled feet. They were men's feet, and I was standing on a flagstone floor. The next sensation was the feeling of a rough cloth against my skin. I realised it was a monk's habit. I spent a while exploring my surroundings. I saw a large monastic building with very little adornment, with stone columns running either side of a central isle, and a large, colourful stained glass window at one end. As I looked to my left I could see a cloistered walkway with open views over a mountainous terrain. Warm sunshine was flooding in from this side of the building and throwing huge shadows over the floor of the nave. I caught the scent of wild herbs on the breeze. I had the impression I was in the southeast of France. I felt at home in the environment and was happy to explore further when the voice on the tape directed me. I walked towards the stained glass window and turned right through a stone arched doorway. I continued along a dark corridor with heavy wooden doors along the right-hand side. I pushed open the second door and recognized the room I had called my own in this previous life. It was a small room, with only a table and one chair for furniture. In the corner was a pallet of straw that was once my bed. The room was very dark, with one small window heavily shuttered to the outside. A single tallow candle placed on the table was the only source of light. Once again, this did not feel oppressive or uncomfortable; in fact the room had a very calm ambience. I had obviously been happy here.

The voice on the tape then directed me to move forward in time by 15 years; this time I found myself cross-legged on the floor in front of the dazzling stained glass window. I looked up and could see the sun streaming through the small panes of coloured glass. As the light shone through, it was refracted into brilliant rays of brightness. I realised that as an older man I had learned how to 'become' the separate shades. I could meld my consciousness into each vivid shaft of illumination, mixing my energy with that of each colour. I was able to change my vibrational frequency to become *at one* with each separate particle of light. I sat awhile bathing in the colourful energy flow.

Eventually, the tape moved me to the moment of my 'passing' in that lifetime. I looked down at myself lying on my pallet as an old man, with long grey hair and a scruffy beard. Gathered around were my fellow brother monks. It wasn't a sad occasion. I felt no emotional tie to the event, and watched the scene below me quite dispassionately. I knew that it was my time to go and was perfectly happy and ready to move on.

At the end of the tape you are given the opportunity to go back and change any of the events that might have occurred, to alter them to your satisfaction. I'd had a very fulfilled and joyful life and I decided I would change nothing.

I discovered an interesting fact relating to this life years later, when leafing through a book. I read how in medieval times the glass used in gothic churches and cathedrals had a particular luminosity that cannot be reproduced today. It had the capacity to filter harmful UV light, and even in poor lighting conditions it managed to retain a clear radiance. Modern glassmakers have attempted to recreate this phenomenon and failed, it would appear that somehow the secret has been lost. In my current life I am partially colour-blind, (you should see me play snooker) but this was obviously far from the case in this former life.

Sometimes we have 'carry-overs' from a former life. This might manifest itself in a birthmark in an unusual place, which can sometimes be attributed to the cause of a sudden or traumatic death in a former existence. It may show itself in irrational fears or phobias, such as a fear of water or fear of a particular animal.

I have recently recognized that I have a carry-over from my former monastic existence, as the top of my head looks like a poorly made crop-circle. My kids are always telling me "Dad, you've got a hole in your hair." As the years go by, I've resigned myself to the fact that I'm beginning to look more like Ghandi than Gandalf. It's not too bad a burden I suppose, although the constant jokes are a little tiring, and it's hard to keep cheerful when a stranger knocks his pipe out on your head. Why couldn't I have had a more glamorous 'carry-over'? A scar down my face perhaps, given to me by a swarthy pirate after protecting a maiden's honour? Or teeth marks from wrestling lions as a gladiator? I'd even have settled for webbed feet after a life in Atlantis - but no, not me, I have ended up with a terrible monk's hair-do. You could call it a case of 'tonsure-itis'. In fact, it could be classed as a 'comb-over' from a former life. Still, I suppose it might have been worse, I could have once lived as an Egyptian eunuch.

You can imagine how I jumped for joy when my sister-in-law stated her intention to do a degree in Hypnotherapy, specialising in past-life regression. She said she would need lots of guinea pigs to practice on. I immediately formed a queue on my own and told her I wasn't a guinea pig but a fully-grown man and to 'have a care, strange woman.'

The key to a successful hypnotic regression is relaxation. As I knew the hypno-therapist I was fully confident and trusting in her ability, and soon found myself, once again, exploring a former life. This one felt different immediately. I was stood in the middle of an African village, built into a gentle hillside, with views over open land to the horizon. My skin was jet-black, and I could feel the earth beneath my bare feet. One of the first things that struck me was the shape of the houses, which weren't the typical mud and straw shaped huts you normally associate with this part of the world. They were made from hard clay and were tall and conical in shape, with the odd one or two being flat roofed with a castellated edge. My role in this village was as an assistant to the local shaman, or healer. He was a small, older man with huge playful eyes and a big toothless grin. My job was to mix leaves and herbs together as potions. I watched as he applied a poultice to a ladies arm, smoothing the mixture to a paste over her forearm, and then wrapping and binding it tightly with leaves. I asked the shaman his name. "Ratatm" he said then fell about laughing. To this day I don't know what he found so funny. Perhaps it's a rude word in African. I might have seen the joke if he'd said his name was Trevor or Bernard.

I was soon asked to progress forward 15 years in this life. I was immediately aware that people surrounded me. They were dressed in the most vibrant coloured garments, a veritable sea of colour, and were all walking towards a huge walled town. The outer wall was about 30 feet high, and the people around me were all funnelling towards a large gated entrance. The cacophony was incredible; singing, shouting, animals shrieking. The general air of excitement and anticipation was tangible. My sister-in-law asked me if I knew the name of this town. Instantly, without having to think, I said Timbuktu. I have no reason for this, and to be honest, at that time I couldn't even be sure if Timbuktu was in Africa. Presently I continued on into the town itself.

The street was lined with stalls selling all manner of exotica, including cloth, spices, and sandals etc. I managed to thread my way through the maze of people until I was approaching a substantial, central citadel. There was a large, arched passageway that was built into the side of the wall, and as I walked along it the sounds from outside faded. The further I walked the darker and cooler it became.

At the end of this passageway was a door, guarded by two men dressed in white. They acknowledged me and opened the door. Once inside, the heavy wooden door was bolted behind me. The room I had entered was small, whitewashed and had a vaulted ceiling. Around the edge of the room were 7 or 8 men sat with their eyes closed, and they appeared to be meditating or praying. In the centre of the room was a plinth with a stone bowl on top. The bowl contained grey ash, which was smouldering and emitting a strong scent. My sister-in-law asked me if I knew my reason for being there. I carried a small satchel bag over my shoulder, and I was delivering something to these men. I took out a metallic object in the shape of a large horn. What struck me as unusual was that it seemed chromed, which appeared wholly out of place in these surroundings. The item was handed over and I left the room. Once again, I was projected forward another fifteen years.

I was standing alone in an open piece of countryside. There was nothing around me but rocks and scrubland, and I could feel the searing African heat rising from the ground. I was aware that above me was a spinning vortex of light filling the whole sky. I knew it was some kind of craft. As this point in the regression I felt my logical mind kick in. 'This is ridiculous,' I said to myself, 'You are making this up.' I knew how far-fetched the situation sounded, so I decided not to repeat what I was seeing for fear of ridicule. I kept it wholly to myself, and I continued the regression until its natural conclusion.

A few weeks later I shared the whole story with a friend, minus the vortex of light incident. "I believe Timbuktu is in Mali," she said. "They have a very interesting tribe called the Dogon. I have a film of them somewhere." We watched the film and the villages were exactly as I had described them from memory, including some peculiar shaped buildings that, according to the film, were millet stores – this being one of the staple diets of the Dogon. The film revealed that they now export a large amount of millet for bird feed, but also as a supposed cure for baldness! After the film finished my friend stunned me with another piece of information. "The Dogon have a history of encounters with extraterrestrials." she revealed, "Apparently they knew about Sirius B, a star invisible to the naked eye long before powerful telescopes discovered it." I was stunned. Convinced I had imagined the spinning lights – was new evidence now suggesting I hadn't?

***

Of course, many of us would like to think that in a previous life we have been somebody wildly exotic or of worldly importance; at the very least a Pope or Egyptian Pharaoh. Heaven only knows how many people have laid claim to having been Cleopatra or Napoleon. It's an attractive notion for people who haven't achieved what they would have desired in this life. I had an experience of this at a past-life workshop I attended, which was made up of an eclectic mixture of people, from young to old-aged and middle-aged to New Age. One man had a bright orange Mohican, a bit unusual for a pensioner, but hey, this was Cornwall..

We were taken through a relaxing guided meditation. In a room full of strangers, and sitting very quietly, I can't help but think inappropriate thoughts to myself. There is nothing worse then knowing you are not meant to laugh. Fighting the urge to giggle, I tried to concentrate and pretty soon found myself in a shallow hypnotic state. The lecturer approached each person in turn and asked them what they could see. True to form, most recollections were of ordinary lives. There were soldiers from all periods of history and men and women working in service. Some people had no recollections at all.

The teacher came over and placed his hand on my shoulder. Here was my big moment. Stand well back! "Tell me where you are and what you see," he said.

Cor blimey Mary Poppins, I was a chimney sweep! Can you believe that? A bloody chimney sweep! I wanted to be a vicious Viking warrior called 'Thor the Magnificent'- but no, instead of carrying a broadsword dripping with blood, here I was with a set of excessively large brushes slung over my shoulder and a face full of soot. Making a sweep exotic was even beyond the powers of Dick Van Dyke. Worse was to come; as I talked through this life it came to light that I used to steal from my clients. I wonder if this explains my current fascination with Toby jugs and pocket watches.

Most people discussed their experiences calmly, until the teacher approached one lady. I had spotted her as we had entered the room. She was already seated and had the look of a communist dictator surveying her minions. It was a look that said, *a great one is amongst you and you don't know how lucky you are!* She was all fake fur, attitude and dirty blond highlights.

"Tell me where you are and what..."

"I AM VESUVIUS MAXIMUS," she roared, jumping to her feet. "AND I DEMAND RESPECT. I COMMAND LEGIONS OF MEN AND I WARN EACH AND EVERY ONE OF YOU THAT I DO NOT SUFFER FOOLS GLADLY." Her voice was now rattling the light fittings, but she wasn't finished yet... "I HAVE FOUGHT MANY BATTLES FOR MY EMPEROR AND NEVER BEEN BEATEN."

I was shaken out of my reverie and opened one eye to sneak a look. She was standing with her hands on her hips, her head thrown back and her chest puffed out, looking for all the world like a second-rate Mussolini. What an actress, I thought. Is she Russell Crowe's auntie? She stood in silence for a few minutes looking down her nose. Was she waiting for applause? I think she was hoping that the tutor would recognise her greatness and obviously ask her to carry on teaching the workshop. He looked thoroughly unimpressed. The expression on his face said, *I've seen it all before*.

"How very interesting..." he said flatly, quickly moving on to the next person. The lady realised she'd been rumbled. Red faced she sank heavily into her chair.

As we chatted at the end of the workshop, the teacher explained that more information might come to us over the coming days and weeks. I was prompted to share my own experience of this and told them of my African regression and the subsequent information I received about it afterwards.

At the close of the evening a strange vision made its way towards me. A man of around 60 came and sat by my side. He was wearing a bright purple shell suit, set off with brown brogue shoes and white socks. He was sporting a wonderful 1980s bubble perm that made him look like an ageing Kevin Keegan.

"You like to beam me up Scottie?" he asked me. I looked around for Matron...

"Star Trek you are liking?" He turned out to be a German gentleman, and my story had intrigued him. He was asking if I was a fan of Science Fiction. He seemed disappointed when I told him that it wasn't really my cup of tea. I also wondered if it would be prudent to warn him that Daleks came out of household plug sockets. However, appearances can be deceptive, and he turned out to be an interesting and polite man. Once again I had been quick to judge somebody by appearance alone without bothering to listen to the content of what they had to say, as before when I had scoffed at the lady doing the 'angel workshop' and she had kindly told me I was to write a book. It did cross my mind that this might be a personality trait I've brought over from another lifetime. We sat and talked for over thirty minutes and he displayed a broad knowledge on many subjects. Truth be told I could have talked for longer but he was called away. The message I took away with me wasn't, *never judge a book by its cover*, but rather *never judge an owner by his shell-suit.*

***

'False Memory..!' I can hear my sceptical father crying. He would claim that recollections during regression are all made up by the sub-conscious. Or even more bizarrely, when details prove historically accurate, that it must be 'inherited memory' passed down from your ancestors through your genes. If this was so, surely you could only inherit the memory of someone up to the point of birth, after this point you can no longer acquire any information genetically. How can people under hypnotic regression give an account of their whole lives, *including their death?* You can't inherit the memory of someone's death.

For many people, a past life regression session can be a therapeutic experience. Many times it can get to the root of our problems that we may have in this lifetime. They may be issues with relationships, or health problems or irrational phobias. Many of these can be traced back to incidents that happened lifetimes ago and we bring a 'carry over' encoded in our DNA. For example, I can't abide having my feet touched. For a grown man I also have very small feet. I was having some healing on my back once from a very well respected Reiki master and clairvoyant, when she said, "You don't like having your feet touched do you?" I replied that she was correct, I couldn't stand it. "I know why," she continued, "Your feet were once tightly bound. You were imprisoned and hung up by your feet, and I can see it all in my mind's eye. I bet you hated being lifted up by your feet as a child," How right she was, it scared the living daylights out of me.

Regression can shine a light into the dark corners of our subconscious mind and help to begin to unravel many problems. Personally, I always find it nothing but positive and feel a more rounded and complete person for having experienced it. It can bring about a new understanding of ourselves and make us see 'living' in a whole new light. Some people even report having found new talents that have lain dormant for lifetimes. This might manifest in a sudden rediscovery of a musical talent or artistic flair.

So the question now is – who do you think you were?

***

It was a proud moment as Barry, the market manager, presented me with my high visibility fluorescent jacket. A sleeveless monstrosity the colour of out of date Lucosade, with the words "Fire Officer" emblazoned on the back.

"Nick, this is a responsible position, so do me a favour and no sodding around, ok?" he said firmly.

"Who me? Sod around?" I asked with all the innocence I could muster, "Me, sod around? As if..."

This had all come about as the result of an inspection by a local fire chief. One of the fire doors is directly next to my unit, and so my close proximity to it, rather than any admiration for my responsible nature, meant that the honour of "fire guardian" fell at my feet.

"Mummy and Daddy will be so proud of me!" I said to Barry as he handed me my jacket.

Barry was a huge man, well over six feet tall and weighing in at a colossal thirty stones He loomed large over the market in the manner of a Regimental Sergeant Major " Your main job is to see that all exits are kept clear and that people know where to assemble in the event of a fire."

I saluted, "SIR!" I yelled and clicked my heels together.

*"At least **try** and take it seriously, will you," he pleaded.*

The next Saturday a memo was sent round informing all the stallholders that the following day a practice drill would take place. The word PRACTICE was in bold letters. The chief fire officer was coming along and all was to run smoothly.

I immediately hatched a cunning plan to add some realism to the proceedings. My good friend John runs a stall selling Army and Navy surplus: an Aladdin's cave of camouflage nets, rope, camping stoves, second hand battledress, inflatable life rafts, etc.

"John, I've got a good idea...."

And lo, the great day dawned. At nine thirty sharp (halfway through my egg bap) the fire alarms sounded. Everyone dutifully shuffled outside and I quickly sprinted to John's stall in order to execute our mission.

Five minutes later the pair of us burst through the fire doors dressed in gas masks and wearing white jump suits, as if attending the clean up at a nuclear spillage. Between us we carried a stretcher, on which was laid a mannequin dummy minus one leg and sporting an ill-fitting wig that looked like road kill.

"Make way," I screamed, "Make way, we have casualties" I was carrying an old-fashioned brass car hooter around my neck. I squeezed the bulbous rubber end and it gave a satisfying honk, like a goose farting in the fog. We rushed to where everyone was gathered and laid the stretcher

down. John produced an old stirrup pump and proceeded to try and resuscitate the corpse.

"Nick, it's not working," he yelled, "We're losing him."

"Not while I'm on duty we're not!" I screamed. "I can save him, because..." here I paused for dramatic effect and put on my best Billy Connolly accent, "I AM AN AROMATHERAPIST! Quick someone fetch me some Aloe Vera and a vial of lavender water."

All at once the world seemed to darken as if a storm cloud had passed over the sun, throwing the world into shadow. I turned to see the huge bulk of Barry looming over me, his face purple with rage; as was that of the fire officer behind him...

I escaped with my life, but he did confiscate my bucket of sand for a week.

***

Chapter 6

ALL I HAVE TO DO IS DREAM

'You don't have to be miserable to be serious'

Eric Morecombe

It took six strong men to lower Barry's coffin into the ground. He was buried on a windswept Cornish hillside overlooking a wooded valley. As the market manager, I had known him for the best part of twenty years. His sheer size and forceful personality had 'put the wind up me' for years, but it wasn't until I met him socially at a wedding that I saw the other side to his nature. We sat and talked for hours as he regaled me with stories from his life. He was generous, kind (although he would never admit it), intelligent and wickedly funny. Eventually ill health got the better of him and he passed away. As I walked away from his grave with the masses of other people who had turned up to pay their last respects, I never expected to see him again.

How wrong I was, because about two weeks later he came to me in a dream visitation. I was standing in a forest clearing and could see a figure in the distance walking towards me. As he came closer I realised it was Barry, although for the life of me I couldn't work out why he would want to see me. He then did something really strange. He reached up and snapped a branch off a tree and started to jab me in the stomach with it. I can remember feeling each thrust as it hit me. I was fully aware that I was asleep but I definitely had the sensation of touch. Barry was laughing loudly by this point. I asked him why he was doing this, and he replied, "Don't you remember? I was always giving you stick!" And with that he faded away. I remember feeling pleased that he had managed to make such a strong contact, and I was also impressed that in so short a time since his passing, he was capable of amassing the energy that is needed to make this kind of connection.

Visitations have a very different feel to them than ordinary dreams. They hold a certain truth to them and have a 'reality' ordinary dreams don't carry. They tend to contain some unique elements that dreams do not have. Visitations are ordered and straightforward, and they often have a pure simplicity, with none of the jumble and confusion of a normal dream. The element of touch is more apparent, and they feel as if they are actually happening in true reality at that moment. They tend to be very structured with few distractions, and place the emphasis on the interaction between the spirit and the dreamer. Ordinary dreams can so often seem jumbled and random, with the feeling of having no control over what is happening; visitations don't feel like this.

It takes a huge amount of energy for a spirit to communicate in this way, so they may only be able to sustain the visitation for a few moments. I tend to get a lot of my communications in this way, because my subconscious mind is more accessible during sleep. The link is easier to establish for spirit without having to fight its way past the claptrap that fills my brain during waking hours. Visitations can bring comfort and validation for the recipient, but sometimes they can also present us with a unique opportunity to offer *our* help to the spirit realm; even when it comes to animals...

Dilly and I had only been married a matter of weeks when we decided to get a dog. It wasn't, as some people accused us, a surrogate baby; we simply wanted a companion to share walks with and maybe even train to run errands, like doing the weekly shop at Tesco's or mowing the lawn. At the very least we expected it to be able to clean up after itself in the garden. Unfortunately, none of these things materialised – but we loved our puppy all the same.

We had decided that rather than choose some highly-strung pedigree, we would go through the harrowing experience of searching the local rescue centres for mongrels. Our local RSPCA centre was the first call. Some human beings should hang their heads in shame at the cruelty they inflict on other living creatures. The kennels of the rescue centre were crowded with far too many mistreated dogs.

One in particular broke my heart. A small brown bull terrier sat forlornly behind the grey chain-link fence. As we approached he made a huge effort to get up from his bed, but the dog was incapable of walking in a straight line, and kept veering sharply to his right hand side. He would take four steps then stop, readjust the angle of his body to point in the direction that he wanted to go and then continue on his way for another few steps. A sign on the kennel read 'Possible Brain Damage' and the notice went on to explain that the dog had been rescued from a man who had almost kicked it to death. We discussed if we should take him, but in all honesty, the poor animal required constant care. Only an experienced dog handler could give him the love and care that was required to enable him to have a fulfilled life. Two newly-weds weren't the answer for this dog. It struck me as strange that the animal showed no signs of mistrust towards humans; he could hardly walk but his little tail never stopped thumping from side-to-side.

That is why we become so attached to our pets; they show unconditional love to us. Their affection doesn't depend on us flattering them or buying them gifts to show our appreciation. They aren't bothered about our religious beliefs, our political persuasion or the colour of our skin. All they ask in return is the occasional walk, a tin of food and tickle on the tummy.

The next enclosure we came to was full of abandoned puppies. At the sight of two humans, the kennel erupted into a mass of writhing, leaping, yapping bundles of fur, all climbing over one another in an attempt to show off. The excitement was infectious, and the dogs egged each other on to seemingly higher and higher degrees of manic behaviour. To the right hand side of all the somersaulting puppies was a small black Labrador. She was staring at the other dogs with a bemused look that seemed to say, 'Fools, that will never get you a home – watch and learn.' She walked towards us, sat down, and gazed into our faces with a pair of the biggest, pleading brown eyes I have ever seen. She pricked up her ears and put her head to one side,

"I want that one!" Dilly wailed, and promptly burst into tears. "I can't look at any more, she's the one, that little black one, you sort it out – I'm going back to the car."

What a softie! – Letting a few waifs and strays tear at her heartstrings. Not me, I was made of sterner stuff. It would take more than a few abandoned puppies to make me cry. A few minutes later I stumbled ungainly through the door of the main office.

"Waaaah!" I blurted through tear stained eyes to two startled looking women. They were obviously old hands at dealing with over-emotional people and they kindly sat me down and gave me a tissue for my streaming nose. After ten minutes, a few deep breaths and a box of *Kleenex*, I had regained the power of speech and managed a coherent conversation with the members of staff. "I've found a dog that we'd like please." I said. For a small donation to the

RSPCA we got a blue lead, a booklet on fleas, and an adorable small black puppy. We named her Jessy.

Within a matter of days she had made herself part of the family. She laid claim to the three feet of carpet in front of the fireplace, and refused to move even when there was a smell of burning fur. She would sneak upstairs in the dead of night and stealthily climb onto our bed and within seconds be snoring like a walrus with a heavy cold. Any person who left her company for more than five minutes was greeted like a long lost friend on their return. Her tail would wag so furiously that she would flip herself onto her side, whimpering excitedly all the while. Jessy's favourite place, apart from our bed and in front of the fire, was the beach. She discovered early on that it was impossible to bark under water, no matter how hard she tried. When I went surfing we had to make sure she was on a lead, as she would follow me. She would thrash desperately through the breaking waves in a vain attempt to reach me only to be spat unceremoniously back onto the sand, time and time again, by the huge Atlantic breakers.

She remained a constant and faithful companion over many years. Children arrived in the Richardson household, and Jess never showed any signs other than love for them. Her tail frequently knocked wobbly toddlers off their feet. Her ears were pulled, she was poked in the eye by jammy fingers, and her tail was shut in cupboard doors. She took it all in her stride and only ever replied with a good-natured sloppy lick. She saw both our children as a constant source of scraps, and I'm sure she had some psychic ability. She knew when food was about to be dropped; she could be fast asleep in another room, and yet when a piece of toast was carelessly flung from a highchair she would appear in a flash, dive head-long and catch the tasty morsel before it hit the floor. Her mouth was like a galactic black hole, and once food was in its vicinity it could never escape its gravitational pull.

After thirteen fun- packed years, age took its toll. She started to behave in an unusual manner and when left alone in the house she would howl. This then manifested into messing throughout the house, leaving a trail from the front door to the back. This type of behaviour was totally alien to her. At first we denied there was a problem and put it down to her old age. When we did take her to the vets he gave her some tablets for anxiety. These made no difference. Things came to a head one day when I arrived home from work. Dilly met me at the door in tears.

"What ever is the matter?" I asked. The look in her eyes told me I didn't really want to know the answer.

"Jess is not well, come and look," She sobbed. I strode into the house and found her lying down in the kitchen. As I entered, her tail gave a weak but familiar thump on the floor.

"Call her to you." instructed Dilly.

"C'mon mate," I said, crouching down and slapping my hands on my knees. "Come and see your old man." Slowly, she got to her feet and tried to walk towards me, but no matter how hard she tried she couldn't walk in a straight line. Her head kept veering to the right and her body followed. You could see the frustration in her eyes. She knew where she wanted to go, but her legs wouldn't take her there.

"Take her in the garden and watch her outside," Dilly whispered. I opened the door and helped her outside. She was a sorry sight. Head bowed, she attempted to climb a small step but was totally incapable. Her legs wouldn't go where she wanted them to. Once on the lawn, she walked around in endless circles, unable to make the straight line back to the house, until she almost fell down in exhaustion. My mind was cast back all those years to the time when we first got her from the kennels. She moved in the same way as the bull terrier with brain damage.

We knew the end had come for her, but it was still the hardest and most traumatic decision we would ever have to make. She would have to be put down, we knew that, but still found it impossible to accept. She had travelled a long road with us. She'd been with us as newly-weds and first-time house-buyers, penniless and broke. There were many days when she got fed and we didn't – Dilly frequently had to stop me from licking out the dog's bowl! She had shared in the joy and happiness that children bring. Endless hours on the beach, rain or shine, she didn't care.

I clearly remember sitting on the kitchen floor holding her head in my hands and looking into her big brown eyes, and trying to explain to her why we had come to this terrible decision. It was a pretty lame attempt to quieten my own guilt, to try and convince myself that on some level she would understand. I desperately wanted to let her know that we weren't betraying her, even though we weren't entirely convinced of this ourselves.

The next morning we sat quietly in the waiting room at the vets. Jessy lay on the floor at my feet, oblivious to her fate. A lady came and sat opposite and looked over the top of her cat basket at me. She glanced down at Jessy,

"Oh, isn't she lovely, look at her laying there, what a good girl." she offered, probably by way of a conversation opener, but I'm afraid neither Dilly nor I felt very talkative. We both sat trying to keep our minds on other subjects. I dare not think about what we were about to do for fear of breaking down, or worse, picking her up in my arms and making a run for the door.

The vetenary assistant popped her head into the waiting room; she knew why we were there. We both went into the room with her. We had decided that the least we could do was to be with her when she passed. If nothing else, to stop her feeling scared. We couldn't just hand her over to a stranger, shut the door and walk away. We owed her more than that.

The vet reassured us that we were doing the right thing. In our hearts we knew that we couldn't let her suffer. To watch her deteriorate and become even more confused and scared would have been downright cruel. As we picked her up and placed her on the table knowing that this was *it,* we still fought a growing sense of guilt. As the vet prepared the syringe we both walked round the table to where Jessy's head hung limply down and stroked her and talked to her. To shield myself from the coming pain I cast my mind back to when she was a young dog.

We had invented our own unique trick called, 'Up the Jumper.' Jess would sit waiting for my command. At the given cue, she would sprint towards me, running lopsidedly with legs too big for her body and her tongue hanging out. I would lift open the bottom of my old baggy jumper and she would leap up the inside of it, scramble her way to the neck hole and plunge her face through so that both our heads poked out of the one hole. She could never quite get her long tail to behave itself and this was always left poking out from the bottom of the jumper, wagging furiously between my legs. Not the most comprehensive expression of man and dog working in close harmony I grant you. I mean, this was hardly herding sheep, rescuing people buried under avalanches or assisting in drug busts, but we were proud of it.

And I'm convinced it would have secured us at least a semi-final place on Britain's Got Talent.

We held her close and the vet administered the injection. He had assured us that she would feel nothing, but as the syringe was pressed she began to whimper. It was a mournful almost panicky cry, as if she couldn't believe what was happening to her.

We stroked her head and spoke softly to her hoping to calm her fears, but she continued her feeble yelping. It sounded like a cry for help. To our guilt-ridden minds it was as if she couldn't quite comprehend that we had betrayed her.

Eventually, her head flopped down onto the table and she fell silent. Her body lay motionless except for her tail, which continued to twitch with muscle spasms. *That* tail that had been so much a part of her character, it should have been registered as a dangerous weapon. It was ironic that the part of her that always had a life of its own should be the last part of her to stop moving.

The vet said he would leave us alone for ten minutes; he closed the door on our grief as we had closed the door on Jessy's life. We both cried uncontrollably, partly from the obvious loss, but also from the enormous weight of guilt bearing down on us. I can't remember how long we spent stroking Jessy's lifeless form, running our hands over her beautiful coat of glossy black fur that never lost its lustre even as she became grey and old.

Our sons had asked if we would take Jessy's body home and bury it in the garden, but we had decided against this, as we didn't want her grave to be a shrine to her death. The real Jessy wasn't buried under the ground; we knew her consciousness had moved on.

The next few weeks passed by slowly. The house had an empty feeling to it and we frequently found ourselves dangling a hand over the side of an armchair, subconsciously expecting to come in to contact with a pair of warm ears or a wet nose. Walks on the beach weren't half as much fun without the joy of watching Jessy throw herself around in the sea with carefree abandon. Eventually though, the pain eased and life got back to normal.

A few months later we returned to our medium friend Mrs Plum. The anguish of losing our best friend was still there but had been dulled by time.

We both breathed a sigh of relief when Mrs Plum told us she had a black dog in spirit for us. Our relief was misplaced though, as she told us it was a Border Collie.

"No, that's not right." I said, "She was a black Labrador."

"That's not the kind of dog I'm seeing." replied Mrs Plum, "It's definitely a Border Collie, I *do* know my dogs." she emphasised. The greeting we received at her front door was a testament to that statement. We soon realised our mistake – my sister's dog, Billy, had died tragically a few years before Jessy. He was a Border Collie and had lost his life when he was run over by a neighbour's tractor. We asked about Jessy, but she said she couldn't see or sense her. This confused us for some time.

A while later a psychic friend of ours said she had received a message for me to say that Jessy was 'stuck.' Apparently, her soul hadn't fully moved into the spirit realm. This really alarmed me. The guilt of having her put down and the stressful manner in which she died had emotionally injured me and now to find out this news; it felt like the most wretched betrayal.

That evening during my meditation I asked for help. I sent out a plea for assistance that, in some way, I might be able to help Jessy move on. Thank goodness the message seemed to get through, because later that night, I had a vivid dream visitation.

As usually happens to me in this form of communication, the feeling I had was one of a particular type of awareness, neither asleep nor awake, but seemingly fully in control of how I wanted events to be shaped. I was sat on a sofa surrounded by a grey mist. Before long the atmosphere to my right-hand side started to change. The air surrounding me appeared to become lighter and less pressurised and before my eyes Jessy began to materialise. I was totally aware of what was happening and made a conscious effort to try and concentrate my energies into making a link. I reached towards her face and felt the familiar warmth of her ears against my palm. I placed my hands either side of her head and held my face next to hers and I could feel her soft shiny body as distinctly as I could when she was on my own side of life. She felt warm against my cheek and she gave a familiar nudge of her nose to force my hand over her head. I breathed in deeply and realised she smelled the same as she always had – a familiar aroma of digestive biscuits and old blankets. I knew this was my chance to explain to her that she needed to pass on and move forward to where she should be. I reassured her that it was ok for her to go. I held her close to me for a few seconds more and she gradually faded away. I was left with a feeling of contentment and great peace, but I also felt privileged to have been given the chance to share another moment with her, however brief.

***

Remember how when you were young you would sometimes call family friends uncle? Not because they were blood-related, but because occasionally friendships can be closer than any family ties. A close 'uncle' of mine in his mid sixties died unexpectedly. The shock came from the fact that he was so *alive*. His own father had lived well into his 90s and I somehow supposed that he too would make old bones. He'd been an integral part of my life growing up. He would enchant us for hours with his seemingly never-ending catalogue of tales and legends. He was a gangly man, well over 6 foot tall, and when he laughed his arms and legs would shoot out in different directions seemingly out of control, and his knees would end up around his ears with his elbows dragging on the floor.

His daughter and I had been best friends since infancy, as had both our mothers before us, but it was this uncle who instilled in us both a deep regard for all things mystical. He taught us never to take anything at face value, to question everything, and to look at life from different angles and perspectives. He was the first person I ever heard talk about spirit guides; I was quite young when he told us of an aunt of his who was very spiritual. One day she glanced in a mirror only to see the face of a Native American staring back at her. I'd never heard about, much less even thought about, anything as bizarre as spirit-guides. He then spent hours filling us in on the subject. He had the happy knack of being able to convey the most incredible tales and make them sound perfectly natural and acceptable.

I couldn't accept that a man so full of life could die so unexpectedly. After he died, he occupied a large amount of my waking thoughts, so I shouldn't have been surprised when one night, when the sub-conscious part of my brain was 'open-for-business', he visited me in a dream. I was alone in the lounge of his house. I heard the door open and he popped his head around it and smiled at me. As he walked towards me I asked him, "Do you know you are dead?" He smiled, nodded and greeted me with a warm hug. I can remember thinking 'Oh my God, I can physically feel you!' He took hold of my hand and placed it on his beard, as if to reassure me that he was fine,"Don't be so intense," he said kindly, "I didn't laugh enough when I was on your side, but *here* it's great, I can do anything I want, I can even fly. Cheer up you big cuckoo and get over yourself." At this point he started to leap around the room ecstatically. He looked not unlike John Cleese with a wasp in his pants, his arms and legs pumping up and down and coming out at right angles.

"I've never felt so alive!" he chuckled.

I laughed and laughed. He wasn't dead, far from it! I woke up with tears streaming down my face, and found it even funnier when awake. (Dilly, however, wasn't so amused to be woken at 3 o'clock in the morning by her husband, braying like a donkey.)

So okay – this was just a dream. But I know with absolute certainty this was no ordinary dream. This was an altered state of consciousness. I knew I was not awake, but I also knew I could distinctly feel the bristles of his beard, and I was fully aware and in control of my mind. My sense of touch and smell were heightened, this was lucid. I'm sure my brainwave patterns had changed from a sleep state vibration to a higher frequency allowing this communication to take place.

Since this first time he has visited me again. This time he was with his father, who was one of the nicest men I have ever known, who enriched the lives of everyone who met him. They were both dressed in white open necked shirts, looking fantastic and radiating health and well-being. They looked like a couple of Greek gods. I was so pleased they'd come to see me again, in fact, I felt quite honoured. We chatted for a while until they indicated that they had very important business to attend to and they had to leave. They smiled, waved, and sprinted away like athletes. I awoke and was left with the most beautiful feeling of calm, serene, happiness. One thing puzzled me - the setting for this encounter appeared to be in a multi-storey car park. I pondered on this for a while and came to the conclusion that this was their way of showing me that there are many different levels to the spirit world. We had met on my level, but where they were going was a place I couldn't follow, the upper levels. Their important business was obviously *up there*.

***

Visitations have a number of key aspects that identify them, and people who share their visitation-dreams are surprised by the similarities in structure, and in the

characteristics that make up a 'classic dream visitation.'
Here are a few points that seem to crop up frequently:

- ◆ Somebody who has passed over will walk into your dream. You immediately realise they are dead and ask them if they know that they are dead.

- ◆ They do know!

- ◆ You are in a bright, fairly plain and uncluttered room, with maybe a couple of chairs or other simple furniture.

- ◆ You might be outside but the landscape is uncomplicated.

- ◆ You might be in a multi-storey car park or other building that has different 'levels.' The deceased person may have come down to your level, or you may have travelled up a level to meet them, but there will be higher levels that are 'out of bounds.'

- ◆ A barred gate or a closed door could also represent 'Out of bounds'.

- ◆ Sometimes you are aware of another 'living' person in the room, and often, though not always, they are unable to see the deceased.

- ♦ The deceased person asks why you or family members are crying.
- ♦ They assure you that they are fine, happy, or well and healthy again now.
- ♦ Your visitation has a vivid clarity you can remember on waking.

Of course there are many variations on these themes, but the format is surprisingly similar. A loved one or friend really has stepped in to your dream state to reassure you that they are fine!

Jessy hasn't fully gone out of our lives even now. Only recently as Dilly was scanning the bookshelves for some reading material, she chose an old book on reincarnation, opened the book at a random page, and started to laugh.

"What are you giggling at?" I asked.

"Have a look." she replied, offering the book to me at the page she had opened. The chapter was entitled *'Animals and Reincarnation.'* Standing out clearly against the white paper background were three huge black Jessy hairs

***

Six months passed before Jack Bell reappeared. He walked unsteadily towards me looking as if he'd recently been knocking loudly at death's door. His glasses sat lop-sided on his face, his tongue hung limply from one side of his mouth and made him look like he was sucking a sock. His coat was slung loosely over one shoulder and dragged along the floor behind him. He looked as if he'd been hit by a tram.

I wasn't alarmed; this was always the way Jack made his entrance; pretending to be on point of death. People queuing to see me looked on in horror. He sat down heavily clutching his heart and panting loudly. I think he may have picked up these acting skills from Shirley MacLaine. They were very convincing and never failed to gain him a seat on buses or in crowded cafes. On a few occasions it had even been rewarded by the offer of a free cup of tea, manna from heaven to any self respecting Yorkshireman. I found this mischievous side of Jack's character very appealing, and played along with it, offering to fetch him drinks or on a few occasions a cylinder of oxygen. I always stopped short of offering the kiss of life' though.

Although he still owned a house in Yorkshire, Jack spent his life roaming the roads of Britain in his caravan. I hadn't seen him in a while and was excited by this theatrical re-entrance into Jacks world. After all, time spent with Jack was anything but dull. After two cups of coffee and three blueberry muffins Jack seemed suitably recovered.

"Nick, I wondered if you would do me a favour?" he asked. My mind went into 'panic-mode' overdrive. Oh god, I hope he doesn't want me to wash his underwear, I thought, they'd have to be done at the jet-wash. Or even worse take him shopping to pick out new ones. No, I could discount this last option as it involved him spending money.

"Would you mind helping me clean out my caravan," he said, "Only it's getting a bit much for me." Relieved, I instantly agreed without giving it much thought. After all, how untidy can one small caravan get...?

I arrived at Jack's the next day, armed with a large roll of heavy-duty refuse sacks and some marigold gloves. Jack was waiting at the door as I pulled alongside.

The caravan was an ancient one. What had once been a white roof was now camouflage patterns of old moss and algae, giving the appearance of a scruffy roof garden. Bits of rusty chrome trim hung haphazardly around its doorway and wheel arches. One window was boarded over with a panel of plywood that said 'Produce of the Windward Isles' in faded lettering. The whole caravan looked as if it had been lifted from an abandoned allotment and deposited by hurricane into this muddy corner of a farmer's field.

"Thanks for coming lad." Jack said with a smile. "I'd normally ask the cleaner, only it's her day off!" He

stepped down from the doorway and I got my first peek inside. During the night an unseen hand must have picked up the caravan and shacken it violently for ten minutes, because the whole area was festooned with junk. The floor (if there was one) was covered in faded newspapers. These were also strewn over the benched seating area. I couldn't see a bed and so I presumed Jack either slept here, under the newspapers, or upright in a cupboard. A yellow bucket sat forlornly in one corner, curtained off from the rest of the van; I could tell from its half full contents that this was the toilet area.

Ultimately, it was quite a sad day. Jack told me how, years before, his wife had died, and after the funeral he had just locked up the house and left, never to return. He couldn't face it; it was too full of memories, too painful to sort through her belongings and discard them. That would mean admitting she was gone. And so he travelled form place to place, year after year, pretending that he still had a wife and home to go back to. He produced a faded photograph from his inside pocket, which looked to have been taken in the 1950s. It showed two people in the prime of life. Jack was looking very dapper in a sharp pinstripe suit, crisp white shirt and matching tie and handkerchief. With his neatly folded Macintosh draped strategically over one arm, he seemed every inch the handsome matinee idol. His other arm was placed lovingly around his wife, who looked as if she was ready for breakfast at Tiffany's. It looked to have been taken in New York.

After two hours we had the van into some kind of order, but I couldn't get over what we had taken out. There were the usual bags of general refuse, but what truly astounded me were the two dustbin bags full of jars of Frankfurter sausages, and four dustbin bags full of cheese! Slab after slab of cheese had been taken from every part of the van, under seats, in cupboards, on surfaces, in boxes, in supermarket bags and behind cushions.

"I like a bit of cheese." Jack said by way of an explanation.

"A BIT?" I bawled, "Jack, this amount would constitute a European Cheese Mountain!"

It was all out of date, most of it by years. Some of it was so old that it had decomposed into lumpy, oily syrup, confined within its plastic wrapping.

"I tend to buy it when it's on offer," he said, "never let a bargain slip by lad. And I'll give you another tip an' all," his eyes brightening. He took hold of one of the dozens of jars of Frankfurter sausages, and cradled it as if it were a Ming vase. "Always keep one of these in your suitcase; you'll never go hungry again. Every hotel room has a kettle, simply boil up the water, pop in four or five sausages, and in no time you'll be dining like a king, and think of the money you'll save on all that crappy hotel food."

Jack seemed perfectly happy with the way he lived, but I was more than a little concerned. He was in his 70s, and Cornish winters can be awfully wet and windy. I knew he had money. Only recently he had shown me a letter from his solicitor informing him of an offer to purchase one of his many business interests. It was a substantial amount, enough to purchase a small house.

"Jack, you don't have to live like this you, know," I ventured cautiously, pointing an accusing finger at the van, "Why don't you spend the winter in a nice hotel or guesthouse?"

A look of both surprise and alarm crossed his face.

"Live like what?" he shouted accusingly. "Who the hell are you to tell me how I should live? What's it to do with you? I'm very happy the way I am, mind your own bloody business."

Oh dear, I had woken the beast. Light blue touch paper and retire, I thought. I had been firmly put in my place and I never broached the subject again. One should never poke a hornet's nest. After loading my car with bags of cheese and other refuse, you can only image the smell.

Jack put his hand on my shoulder, "Thanks for your help lad, it's very much appreciated." We stood smiling at one another, I felt good about having helped an old friend. Although it was a dirty and smelly job, he really couldn't have managed it on his own. "Right," *he said with* enthusiasm, "Let's tidy out my car now, shall we..?"

***

Chapter 7

TALL STORIES AND TINY TEMPLES

Nick would do better in class if he didn't insist

on playing the class buffoon.

School report circa 1979

Although I spent my formative years in a small village in Staffordshire, Cornwall has always been my spiritual home. A trip to Cornwall always felt like travelling abroad, because it was so completely different to everything I had grown up with. It had the obvious attractions of the beach and sea, but I was also drawn to its wild and untamed beauty. On any given day you could be burning the soles of your feet in scorching sand, and the next day you might find yourself nailing your boots to the floor to prevent being blown to northern France via the help of an Atlantic low pressure front. It also smelt different to anywhere else I knew, and the air tasted clean and fresh. But what made it a truly exotic paradise to me was the fact that it had palm trees – which in my book made it positively sub-tropical.

As a young boy, the highlight of the year was always our annual holiday in Cornwall. My father always insisted on travelling through the night in order to avoid traffic congestion, even though my sister said it was because I was so ugly that my family were embarrassed to be seen in daylight with me. In all, the journey took around eight hours, and I would make sure that I stayed awake the whole time because I didn't want to miss a minute of it. Everywhere seemed so different in the dead of night. Brightly lit towns would pass by my window one after another as we made our slow progress southwestwards. We avoided motorway driving where possible and each county border we crossed was greeted with growing excitement. Worcestershire, Gloucestershire, and Avon - they all seemed so exotic to my young mind, almost as if each was an independent foreign land. Passing through Bristol in the deepest hours of the night always afforded us our first view of anything that remotely resembled the sea. The docks lit the night sky with a blaze of colour and could be seen for miles around.

Eventually, after what seemed a lifetime of being sat on a cushion in the front seat, we would stop the car in a suitable layby, as dawn broke over Bodmin Moor. My father would then take out a small camping stove from the boot, and in the early morning light, he would cook us bacon and eggs. This was real adventure; to me this was man's stuff – out in the wilds with the only noises being the occasional bleat from a far off sheep or a single bird clearing its throat ready for the dawn chorus, the lovely sizzle of half a pig frying in the pan, and the mournful grunts of my sister snoring away in the back seat, the lazy cow. How could she sleep through this? Didn't she know what she was missing? Look how big the sky was; it went on forever. High above me the stars still shone clearly in a blue-black sky, but out to the east daybreak slipped silently into the cool air. The first few rays of sunshine peeped cautiously over the horizon and held the promise of a day on the beach in just a few hours time. The light of dawn is so full of hope and she was missing it. By the way she was dribbling I think she was dreaming of David Essex. I liked the fact that it was just me and my dad doing the 'manly' thing and providing food for our two sleeping beauties. It was also our chance for a bit of male bonding, and an opportunity for a crafty wee together behind a convenient stone wall. After all there's nothing like splashing your boots to a good view, and oh, how the mist rose on those mornings.

This was also a great opportunity to ask some of life's big questions of my father, I steered clear of my earlier 'what happens when we die' question this time, and instead plumped for those other conundrums of life that had been bothering me like, 'Why do women's shirts have buttons on the opposite side to men's?' 'Was Asterix the Gaul a real historical figure?' 'What's a jockstrap?' 'Who *was* Gordon Bennet?' and 'Have you ever seen a blue-arsed-fly...?'

I loved the accent of the people in this region. It was soft and rounded and, when spoken quickly, as incomprehensible as any foreign language. Old folk had colour in their cheeks, not like the ones at home whose pallor was ashen grey all year round. The lady who owned the guesthouse where we stayed reminded me of a friendly aunt from the *Famous Five* books. She always wore a powder-blue tabard covered in flour and she smelt of coal-tar soap and medicated toilet paper. I loved the novelty of sleeping in a strange bed with a lumpy mattress, falling asleep to the distant sound of waves breaking, to feel sand in the bed-sheets because I hadn't washed between my toes properly, to awaken to the sound of gulls screeching and crying overhead, goodness me, life is just so uncomplicated when you're 8 years old.

Back at home, I became so obsessed with this idyllic part of the country that I actually placed my bed so that it aligned itself in a south-westerly direction and I would fall asleep knowing that I was facing Cornwall. On the wall next to my bed I had hung a cheap and tacky smugglers map. Emblazoned across the top were the words 'A Souvenir of Cornwall' and I would mark off all the places we had visited in bright orange crayon. By the time I was a teenager I would cycle the two miles to the A38 duel carriageway that ran alongside our village and spend my evenings on a bridge looking down on the cars travelling southbound. It may have been hundreds of miles away but I knew this road could take me to Cornwall. To me it represented freedom – a means of escape.

It could be called fate, destiny, creating your own reality or just luck, but years later, when the chance to move to Cornwall came along, my wife and I grabbed it with both hands. We had only been married for 18 months, and were just starting out on our life together, but the opportunity was too good to miss.

My sister had moved to Cornwall through her husband's career and had invited us down for the weekend. At this time my wife was working for national children's wear retailer, and whilst we were walking through the local town I joked that; 'wouldn't it be funny if they were advertising her current position in the window of the local branch?' To our utter amazement and glee, they were! My wife wasted no time in speaking to the manager, who was more than happy to take on a person who would need no training and was already an employee of the company. A quick call to head office, and within minutes the position was hers. It all seemed so easy. I was self-employed and so upon returning home I immediately placed my business up for sale, and within weeks we were living in Cornwall

Suddenly I realised what it felt like to be alive, rather than to just exist. Dilly and I spent hours walking the cliff-tops and put hundreds of miles on the car exploring the county's back roads. Wherever you travel in Cornwall there is a palpable sense of its history. It still retains that feeling of being an ancient place. Folklore of Pirates, lost Celtic tribes and the Arthurian legend only add to its mystique. For thousands of years Cornwall's shores have been visited by countless numbers of foreign travellers. Its wealth of natural minerals means that it has always been a trading area. From as long ago as the Phoenician times (available at good newsagents for 50p a copy) Cornwall has been a significant importing and exporting hotspot. It is widely rumoured that Joseph of Arimathea (or as a friend of mine once called him 'Joseph of Aromatherapy!') was a regular visitor to these shores in his capacity as a trader of tin and other goods. Egyptians, Greeks and Asian traders have been visiting here for centuries so it is not uncommon for Cornish folk to have been used to dealing with people of different cultures and ethnic diversity. Cornish people have often been accused of being insular; their history would suggest they are far from it.

The Cornish don't consider themselves to be English; they regard their nationality in the same way as the Welsh and the Scots, and being stuck out into the Atlantic ocean on a rocky peninsular, means that Cornwall feels a long way from the rest of the country. That isolation has created self-sufficiency. People down here don't feel the need to follow the latest trends. The Cornish aren't impressed by status symbols and they don't go in for social climbing. Don't get me wrong and think that they are a dour and humourless lot, far from it; I've always found them open, funny, honest and self-deprecating. You never feel afraid to truly be yourself down here and these people don't feel threatened or embarrassed by self-expression. The openness of their landscape is reflected in the openness of their attitude.

I was reminded of this general acceptance to anything different when I attended a Native American healing circle at a Mind, Body and Spirit Fair. This was a re-enactment of a traditional ceremony and around forty of us sat in a large circle. Our master of ceremonies was a guy called Simon, a tall, thin man with long silver hair and weathered features; he wouldn't have looked out of place living in a tepee. He is well known locally as a powerful healer and channel for spirit. For around 40 minutes he went through an authentic demonstration of the processes and rituals used by Native Americans using chanting and drumming. I found it mesmerizing and powerful, and when I glanced around the room other people seemed as captivated as me; Simon held them spell-bound.

I was struck by the appearance of one young lady. She looked to be in her early 20s and was dressed in dark clothing, and she sat with her head bowed and her arms folded protectively across her chest. She was watching intently, but her body language suggested trepidation to fully commit. After a while Simon led the group through a guided meditation, after which he suggested that we split into groups of four people and give healing to one member of the group. I looked over to the young girl who was sat quietly on a chair while three people stood around her giving her healing. At first she sat with her head down and her arms once more folded across her chest, but after around 10 minutes I noticed that her demeanour had become much more open. Her hands were now placed in a relaxed manner on her lap and she sat with her head up and her eyes closed.

Soon afterwards Simon suggested passing around a 'talking-stick.' My first reaction was to laugh, a *what?* Once again I was proved wrong – the *stick* was just a plain old piece of wood, but it was what it represented that was important. Whoever holds the stick is the only person allowed to speak. It is forbidden to talk unless it is in your possession. This gives a sense of power to the holder – knowing that they will be listened to in full, and not interrupted. The stick was passed from person to person, and Simon had warned us not to spend the time waiting for the stick to come to us worrying about what we were going to say, but to sit and listen to the person talking and to give them our full attention. When the stick was passed to the girl in the dark clothes she looked like a completely different person to the one who had walked into the room earlier. She took the stick willingly and stood up, her voice was loud and clear and she spoke with confidence, looking around the room and engaging with everybody,

"I'm not a local." she began, "this is the first time that I have sat in a room full of people and not been intimidated. I've always felt the need to explain and defend my beliefs. People have always made fun of the way I look and the clothes I wear. I haven't felt that here today. Nobody has judged me or made assumptions based on how I look. For the first time I can actually be *me,* the real *me,* and I've realised today that it's *ok* to be me."

I wondered how long she had felt disenfranchised. How long had she denied her true feelings? How long had she been afraid to be herself because of the worry of others ridicule? She left the meeting totally empowered and I felt it was worth going just to witness somebody's life being transformed. Of course I can't claim that this transformation came about purely because this girl visited Cornwall, it could have happened anywhere, but it *was* dependent upon her perception of how other people viewed her, and I do believe that people living in Cornwall have an inbuilt laid-back attitude to life. And let's get it straight here – laid-back does not mean lazy; laid-back means the ability to not let stress rule your life.

***

At every turn Cornwall conjures up images of its ancient past. West Cornwall, in particular, is littered with numerous primeval sites: stone circles, standing stones, holy wells (still in use), burial mounds and Celtic settlements abound. Many leylines criss-cross this part of the county and each site has its own story or legend to tell. Many a 'green man', that famous pagan fertility deity, can be found in Cornish churches. I have also spotted many a 'green man' stumbling off a pleasure boat after a particularly challenging fishing trip.

I enjoy living in a place where legends and folklore are part of the social fabric. Druids are alive and well here. Cornwall still holds its *Gorsedd,* a gathering where hundreds of druids meet and choose their bard, or leader, for the year. Helston flora day and the Padstow 'obby oss' (hobby horse) are just two of the county's pre-Christian events that take place every year around the festival of Beltane, in early May.

Not to be outdone in the folklore stakes, my own 'neck of the woods' also has a local legend. Giant Bolster, an ogre so large and fearsome, he would make Shrek look like Julian Clarey. Apparently, he was so tall that he could stand with one foot on St Agnes Beacon and another on Carn Brea; two local hills *five miles* apart (the rumour that he then relieved himself on the village I inhabit between these two points is as yet unsubstantiated).

Bolster supposedly fell in love with the beautiful maiden Saint Agnes. To prove his love she persuaded him to fill up a hole on the cliff-side with his blood. He did this willingly; not knowing the pit was bottomless, and bled to death.

The story is re-enacted every year in a cove near the village of St Agnes on Bolster Day, when a huge effigy of Bolster emerges slowly over the cliffs. He stands around fourteen feet high and it takes four people to control him. A big bushy beard of moss, and wild hair of bracken adds to the wild man image. He appears over the horizon to the sound of a Celtic drumming band before coming to his sticky end. As he falls, children run down the hillside streaming yards of red ribbon to represent Bolster's lifeblood draining away. This event is watched by hundreds of local people.

This, like so many other celebrations, honours the Celtic festival of Beltane. On the night before Bolster's big day, a procession of lanterns winds its way through the dusk to the top of the Beacon, where a huge bonfire is lit. People turn out in droves and climb the hillside in the dark to celebrate next to the roaring flames. The pagan isn't very far under the surface of people in this region.

Giants abound in Cornish folklore. Another supposed to live on St Michaels Mount. Interestingly, when excavations were carried out on the island, the remains of a 7ft skeleton were uncovered. Big even by today's standards, in days gone by this man would truly have been considered a giant, especially as the average height of a Cornishman in those days was only 2'4". They used to live in pasties, not eat them.

Many of Cornwall's sacred places pre-date Christianity, but the early Christian church absorbed some of those pagan ideas into its own traditions. The Merry Maidens stone circle near Penzance is a good example of how the church tried to cover up these pagan beliefs. The stone circle sits in windswept countryside and comprises nineteen standing stones, with many of them relating to the cardinal compass points. According to local Christian custom, these standing stones are all that remain of a group of young maidens who were caught dancing on the Sabbath and therefore turned to stone. Luckily, the local populace haven't been put off by this legend, and on any weekend in Penzance many a 'stoned maiden' can still be found making their way home in the early hours of the morning.

One of my favourite sacred places is Madron Well. When we think of a Well we normally imagine a deep circular hole in the ground surrounded by a small wall, with a rope and a bucket above. In the case of Madron Well it is more of a sacred spring. Fresh water oozes out of the ground in the middle of a tight copse of trees. All around where the water forms a pool, people have hung offerings from the surrounding trees. These might be colourful ribbons, garlands of wild flowers or indeed anything that comes to hand to leave as an offering. Occasionally people will leave prayers written on paper and tied to a branch, or even leave photographs of people who need healing. This kind of 'nature worship' has been going on in Cornwall for thousands of years. The spring is situated half a mile down a muddy track, with dense woodland of stunted oak on either side. Within yards of the spring is a disused and roofless single room chapel that only adds to the ambience of the place.

The last time I visited our party numbered around seven people. It was interesting to note that as we walked deeper into the woodland various members began to drop away, saying that it was too far or that the track was too muddy. One person didn't even make it onto the path and insisted on waiting in the car. By the time we reached the spring only four of us remained and we were the only ones interested in the *spiritual* side of life. The seekers, if you like. The others had fallen away from the path, finding it too difficult to complete their journey physically or indeed metaphorically.

They missed out on a magical experience, because as we reached the spring, the sun broke from between the clouds and shone through the canopy of trees. Shafts of sunlight speared around the glade and the whole area became a cathedral to nature. The only noise was that of birdsong and running water. We sat in the old chapel for over an hour. It's a single room building with a small granite slab at one end acting as an altar. The roof is missing and so the sense of space and light is heightened. The old stone walls are covered in moss and create the feeling that the chapel could have grown out of the ground, so naturally does it sit in its wooded environment. Nobody spoke, we didn't need words; solitude and silence brings its own rewards.

**

I like places and events to surprise me, to take me unawares. Unexpected happenings always seem to carry more validity and proof. A strange experience in a remote church was one such example. We discovered the church by accident when we were randomly driving around the deserted lanes of Bodmin Moor, a vast and wild expanse of windswept moorland, open to all the elements that nature can throw at it. This untamed landscape was the inspiration for Daphne de Maurier's atmospheric book *Jamaica Inn,* and it's easy to imagine all kinds of strange and primeval occurrences there. If this were a radio play, this would be the part where the sound effects would be of howling wind, a clap of thunder and a dog baying at the moon. Then a 'salty sea-dog,' voice would rumble.

"Arrrgh, 'twas a dark and stormy night, the wind were crying like a pirate being run through with a blunt cutlass, we was lost on the moor in the dead of night when..."

I wish I could say that my story begins like this, but it doesn't; mine took place on a balmy summers evening.

Temple Church was originally built by the Knights Templars in the middle ages, and the first impression on finding this ancient site is that the landscape probably hasn't changed much in a thousand years, leaving you with the sensation that you are seeing the church through the eyes of its creators. It stands alone and hidden from the worst of the weather in a small valley. It is a simple structure, plain and unadorned. Once inside, the building holds a definite atmosphere. There is an undefined buzz in the air, and perhaps the best way to describe it is by likening it to being in a room where loud music has been playing, when suddenly the volume is turned off and for a few seconds afterwards you can still feel the vibration oscillating in the silence.

My wife and I visited Temple church a few years ago with two friends, one of whom, Meg, was an advanced medium. It was here that we witnessed some unexplained phenomena. As we entered the church I could see that Meg was picking up on the energy, her face took on an excited appearance and her eyes grew brighter. The other three of us meandered around the church admiring the stained glass windows and casting a curious eye over the visitors' book. Meg had wandered away and seemed lost in her own thoughts.

"Okay you three, you need to come over here." she said suddenly. "I've just been told we need to do some earth healing." She was standing alone in the oldest part of the church, which was directly beneath the bell tower. As we joined her she instructed us to stand in a circle and join hands. We did so and Meg offered up a prayer of protection. We stood for 10 minutes in total silence, and then she told us to imagine a huge shaft of light coming down from above, through our circle and shining far down into the earth. It's strange, you would imagine that doing this in a lonely windswept and deserted church would be spooky, but it wasn't in the least. It felt calming and harmonious - a pleasant experience actually. I suppose we stood there for about twenty minutes, but I couldn't say for sure because time had no relevance at that moment. Meg spoke to us throughout, offering guidance and instruction. When we had finished, the four of us went and sat on one of the wooden pews at the front of the church to talk about our experience. As we did so I glanced back to where we had been standing and blurted out, "Oh my God! Look at the floor!" A perfect circle had appeared on the flagstones, almost as if someone had drawn it in chalk over the floor. It was exactly symmetrical, clearly defined and glowed very faintly. Around the edge of the circle we could see the imprints of where our feet had been. The footmarks and circle stayed prominent on the flagstones for around twenty minutes and then gently faded away. This served as proof to me that we had truly channelled some kind of energy through our little group. I don't know what that energy was, but I do know it felt harmonious and balanced. We all left feeling rejuvenated. Meg in particular left with a huge smile spread over her face; that was good enough for me.

Since that day I have felt a strong affinity with that humble little church. I return quite often and always have a feeling of belonging and great peace.

The last time I visited that tiny church I took a small detour, found a layby, and just for old times sake took out my old camping stove and frying pan...

.

***

Having felt good about helping Jack tidy out his caravan, a wave of panic swept through me when he stated we should clean out his car. My goodwill took a nose-dive, and I went from feeling like a Good Samaritan to a shot down fighter pilot in one fell swoop; surely we wouldn't uncover any more cheese? But, there was more cheese... lots more cheese... and then some more cheese... and then just a little bit more cheese. I had to physically prise some of it from Jack's grasp; so loath was he to part with it.

"That's still plenty good enough to eat, that," he yelped with tears in his eyes as I wrestled with him to throw away the offending item, which looked as though it had been plucked from the sluice of an operating theatre.

You can only imagine the stench of my car, with bag after bag of rancid cheese in it. Eventually Jack's car was cleared of rubbish and cheese and nestling at the bottom of the boot was what appeared to be a large pizza box, measuring about 2 feet square.

"What's in the box Jack?" I asked flatly, "A quadruple cheese pizza?"

"Ah, now then," he exclaimed, "That lad, is a one-off!" He opened the box and slid out a huge metal disc. "That's a Zildjian symbol," he said, "best symbols in the world. All the top drummers use them, and this one is personally signed by the boss – Armand Zildjian." I knew

what the next words would be, "He were a friend o' mine." Jack's eyes took on a faraway look, and I knew that he was about to regale me with one of his reminiscences. I sat down all ears.

"Whilst staying in the US we became good friends and I spent some time at Mr Zildjian's house. One evening he threw a large barbecue..."

"Did it hit you?" I interrupted. "I get bad tempered when they won't light as well..."

"Shurrup and listen, you daft bugger... It were a massive party, everyone was there, I met Teddy Kennedy, you know."

"As in JFK's brother?" I asked aghast.

"Aye, one and the same... He was a nice lad." This was said with the nonchalance as if discussing a neighbour's child. He continued, "I nearly got meself in trouble though, I started chatting to this one bloke and the subject came round to politics. Well things got a bit heated, mainly because he wouldn't listen to me, and eventually people started to notice the raised voices. Someone came over to us and made an excuse to lead this fella away. Sometime later this lady, who was all big teeth and shoulder pads, said 'Do you know who that was?'

"Who was it Jack, who was it?" I asked impatiently.

"Well, turns out it was Michael Dukakis, who at the time was running as the Democratic candidate for the Presidency." he laughed.

"Oh my God, what did you say when they told you who he was?"

"I told 'em straight, o' course, I said, 'how the bloody hell do you expect me to know who he is – I'm from Bradford!'"

***

Chapter 8

THE ANSWER IS BLOWING IN THE WIND

'Last night I stayed up late playing Poker with Tarot cards, I
got a full house and four people died.'

Steven Wright

It's amazing how the Spirit world tries to connect with us.
They seem to find all sorts of different ways to send
messages. There is the obvious contact, such as through a
medium or ouija boards, and they have also been known to
use radio frequency waves, or white noise, to pass on
messages.

I've always been envious of people who find it easy
to interpret *subtle* messages sent by the spirit world. My
sister-in-law is a case in point. She is fantastic at dream
interpretation, and has the ability to be able to see through all
the surface thoughts and get right to the heart of the matter.
Quite often I'll mention in passing a stupid dream I've had
and within seconds she has come up with a plausible
explanation for it, and as I think back over the dream I
realise that the message she suggests it conveys always
makes sense. (Except from the time I dreamt of a sheep up a
tree - that really stumped her.)

I admit I'm a bit of a 'thickie!' I never seem to get
discreet hints from Spirit. I regularly have to ask them to

give me *obvious* signs to grab my attention. People say: *A nod's as good as a wink*, but not for me; I need a slap around the face!

I'll give you an example; I had been reading a lot about the Indian mystic Sai-Baba; a man renowned for performing miracles, producing objects out of thin air, and appearing in two places, sometimes in different countries, at the same time. I'd read about people who had stayed at his Ashram in India and been totally changed by the effect this happy, peaceful man had on them. He has his followers, and his critics, but I was still unsure and getting a numb bum from sitting firmly on the fence.

I decided to ask Spirit for a sign. Like everybody, I wanted proof. I try to find twenty minutes out of each day to meditate, in an attempt to reach that state of calm neutrality where my mind isn't clogged up by random thoughts. When I first started, I used to get frustrated because I couldn't seem to clear my brain of the scattered thoughts that raced through it. After a while I realised that the best thing was to just accept these thoughts as part of the meditation process, letting them run their course through my head and allowing them to drift away naturally without judgement or pressure. After much practice I found that I could slip away within minutes. Sometimes I spend time enjoying that neutrality, and at other times I use it as an opportunity to 'tune into' the spirit realm and ask for advice and guidance.

'Okay you lot, if Sai Baba is what he claims to be, I need a clear signal, please.'

I let the message go, thought nothing more about it and continued my day as usual. Later that evening I was working on my computer. Suddenly the screen went blank. I did the usual routine: hitting every key very hard, as if this could possibly make any difference. I slapped the monitor; I kicked the plug…nothing. Eventually, I realised what I had been doing wrong. I hadn't sworn at it! Summoning up every rude word and insult I could think of, I let the computer have both barrels in a tirade of abuse…still nothing. I had to admit defeat, and swallow my manly pride. Shamefacedly, I had to consult The Wife, The Oracle, The Seer, She Who Knows All.

"Darling, the computer has crashed on me." I called in my best *innocent-little-boy* voice, that I use on such occasions as this hoping to avoid any blame.

"Oh no..! What have you done now?" came the reply.

I explained that I hadn't done anything, why, I had hardly touched it, I revealed in hurt tones. My wife repeated the process that I had just gone through, hitting, swearing, etc.

"Really, darling," I chastised, "that's not going to do any good now is it?"

She turned to me with eyes ablaze and was about to shoot me down in flames, when the screen began to flicker. It went from black, to grey, and then a purple box suddenly appeared in the middle of the screen and in it were two words:

> ### GURU
> ### MEDITATION

I stared open-mouthed at the monitor.

"Are you seeing what I'm seeing?" I asked. My wife confirmed that she was. I rapidly explained to her my earlier request for a sign.

"Well, that's a pretty impressive way of sending a sign." she said.

I was really quite dumb-founded. Sometimes you try and explain away these happenings as just coincidence or chance. This was more than that. This was a positive affirmation. To me this was proof, in a most unambiguous form. Needless to say I was highly impressed with Spirits use of a modern communication system. No *burning bush* or *angelic visitations* here. This was high-tech stuff.

The words stayed on the screen for a minute or two and then disappeared. We pressed a few more buttons and the computer kicked back into life.

The most important lesson I learned from this was that spirit actually heard me. I got through, they listened and it worked. I now chat to them all the time. I expect I bore them rigid. I quite often imagine them all sat around 'up there', yawning, while I ramble on and on with the inane chatter that passes for thoughts in my head. So far though, my requests for next weeks winning lottery numbers seem to have fallen on deaf ears.

***

In March, my good friend, Martin and his relatives were devastated by a family tragedy. The normal routine of a Sunday morning had been interrupted by a phone call that was to change his life forever.

"Martin, you need to come over to your mother's house straight away." The voice on the phone said. Martin recognised the voice as his stepfather's, but it sounded scared, with a tone to the voice he'd never heard before.

"I'm just preparing the Sunday roast." Martin replied.

"No, leave everything and come over now," the voice instructed, but this time louder and with more urgency.

Martin knew something awful must have happened for there to be such a sense of insistence in the phone call. He rushed to his mother's home, and upon entering, could tell from the atmosphere permeating the house that something terrible had happened. His mother was too shocked to even speak, and so his stepfather imparted the dreadful news; Martin's elder brother, Andrew, had been killed in a traffic accident.

At 28, Andrew was only one year older than Martin, and the brothers had been really close. Andrew had been everything an older brother should be; exciting, protective, and funny. He also possessed the number one element required to be elevated to superhero status; a motorbike. Details of the accident were sketchy, but that didn't matter to Martin. All he knew was that his brother had gone, he'd been snatched away and Martin would never see him again.

The fabric of the family's life seemed to have been pulled apart. Time stood still. Days and nights rolled in to each other, with no recognisable break between daylight and the hours of darkness. Life seemed to be 'on hold', sleep offered no comfort and being awake was too painful a reality to bear.

The funeral offered a semblance of closure, but dulled none of the pain. Hundreds of bikers attended the ceremony and a guard of honour accompanied the hearse on its slow journey to the church.

Martin had his own health problems to worry about. He suffered from kidney failure, and was reliant on dialysis three times a week to keep him alive. He no longer cared about his own condition, and within six months was admitted to hospital. I remember discussing his health with his mother. The pain in her eyes was evident,

"He doesn't want to live," she said, "He's lying in a hospital bed, pleading with me to let him go and be with Andrew."

To this day, I don't know how she found the strength to deal with this situation – losing one son, and then the threat of losing another must have been almost too much to bear.

Martin didn't die. He hung on and his condition stabilised. I think some inner voice convinced him that it wasn't his time to go, that Andrew wouldn't have wanted it, and that his mother needed him. Eventually he was released from hospital and life returned to something resembling normality.

As a close-knit family, the first Christmas after Andrew's death took on a huge significance. It would be a true test of how far they had travelled to overcome their all-encompassing grief. What was needed was a large family gathering. Martin had been saving a special candle to light during Christmas day in memory of Andrew. In the morning the family attended the grave and placed fresh flowers around it. From the grave they travelled on to Uncle Peter's house. Peter and Andrew were two peas from the same pod and had always had a close bond. When they were together, they used to cause mayhem with their practical jokes and their own particular type of humour. They egged each other on to more and more outrageous behaviour.

On arrival at Peter's house, Martin realised he had left his candle at home. He was distraught; he had placed a lot of emphasis on this particular candle; to Martin, it was a *symbolical gesture* meant to include Andrew in the day. Martin couldn't settle, so decided to drive the five miles home to collect the candle.

After lunch the family exchanged presents and Martin placed the candle in pride of place on the mantelpiece. The family were all silent, lost in their own memories as the flame began to burn. But the peace and harmony was soon shattered when the room was suddenly shaken with a loud and raucous farting noise. Amused glances were exchanged and fingers pointed. The culprit was Peter. He came clean, so to speak, by admitting he had been given a 'fart machine' as a Christmas gift. The weird thing was that he didn't actually have it on him at the time. The unit was placed on a nearby coffee table, and Peter insisted vehemently that he didn't have the remote control for it. He stood up and held his arms away from his body, as if to say, 'search me,' but as he did so another loud 'quack' echoed around the room. Everybody burst out laughing,

"Do it again," they cried,

"I'll have a go," giggled Peter, "but I promise you on my life, I'm not doing it." He lifted his leg, and stuck his backside out; a most satisfying raspberry was heard. "Wait, wait I'll try the other leg," suggested Peter. He lifted the other leg, and once again, right on cue, the machine let out a noise as if someone had trodden on a frog. Time after time Peter repeated the trick, always with his hands in full view. By now, tears of laughter were streaming down his face. "Someone else have a go and see if it works for you," he said, " I need to sit down before I fall down."

There then followed the wonderful sight of a room full of people, all dressed in their Christmas finery, leaping around, cocking legs and pushing rear ends in all directions. It was to no avail. Not even a little *tommy-squeaker* was emitted from the machine; it remained silent on the coffee table.

"Come on Peter, get on your feet and try again," they demanded.

"Okay, okay," he said, standing up, "but I don't think it will do it again." He was wrong. As soon as he started to make the required gestures the machine burst into life with impeccable timing, "Andrew would have loved this," shouted Peter over the hysterical laughter. Someone suggested they all stand still for a few minutes, just to prove that it wasn't a random accident. They did so, and the minutes passed without incident. A further ten minutes was spent searching for the machine's remote control unit, but it couldn't be found. They searched high and low, under chairs, down the back of the sofa. Peter was frisked, and thoroughly enjoyed the experience. Everyone searched each other. The television remote was pressed to see if it interfered with the machines frequency – it didn't.

By now the crowd were baying for more, and encouraging Peter to continue his bizarre performance. He willingly obliged, and leapt and pranced around the room, and every time he lifted his leg or pushed out his backside, the machine replied with a perfect trump. After twenty hysterical minutes, everybody was exhausted. Peter sat down hard in an armchair, "I'm pooped," he quipped. Every now and again, he would randomly lift his leg and the machine duly obliged with a series of toots.

The solemnity of the occasion had certainly been lifted. It was the first time in months that any of the family had smiled, let alone laughed out loud. The day had started with sad memories, brought on by laying flowers on Andrews grave, but had ended with wonderful thoughts of how funny Andrew would have found the occasion. It is interesting to note that as soon as Martin blew out 'Andrew's candle,' the fart machine stayed silent. Try as they might it never made another sound, even for Peter. Within five minutes, the remote control was found on top of a high shelf, where no one could have reached it without being spotted.

Martin is in no doubt as to the machine's strange behaviour. Andrew was doing it. It was his way of saying,

'Hey look, it's me, I'm still with you.' The perfect timing of the noises made it impossible for it to have been coincidence as they were synchronised to the split second time and again. Andrew had obviously found a way to manipulate the machine to his will in a manner that was so typical of his personality. This ridiculous episode acted as a catalyst for the whole family and helped immeasurably with the healing process.

This isn't the only time that Andrew has made his presence known. When he died, he left behind a young daughter who frequently stayed weekends at her granny's house. Andrew's mum heard her granddaughter laughing in her room one night, and when she enquired about it the next morning, the little girl replied, "Oh that's just daddy, he comes and tickles me when I'm in bed sometimes and tells me he loves me."

The years have passed and Martin's life has changed amazingly. He had a successful kidney transplant and no longer needs dialysis; he leads a fit and active life, and is the proud father of delightful twin boys. He's come along way from the shadow of the man lying in a hospital bed pleading to die. I like to think that the inner voice he listened to on that occasion was his brother telling him not to give up, that the future held wonders for him.

***

I don't have many claims to fame. I do have a famous folk singer as a customer (sorry, no names. Doctor/patient confidentiality, you understand.) And, whilst earning my living as a DJ in the 1980s, I once signed an autograph as Andrew Ridgley from Wham! Two teenage girls were convinced that I was him and who was I to disappoint them? Ex-England football manager Graham Taylor once nodded hello to me from his Mercedes in a traffic jam, and as if that wasn't enough, ex-400 meter hurdles champion David Hemery once said good morning to me in a hotel foyer, (actually, he asked me to carry his bags.) Apart from these show-stopping incidents, I don't have any claims to fame; or so I thought. Because according to one elderly couple I posses a rare and unique talent that could lead to fame and fortune.

The pair were regular visitors and seemed every inch the classic devoted couple. Both looked well into their eighties, and the gentleman would dutifully push his disabled wife around in her wheelchair.

They arrived one day in high summer. The lady's face was glowing bright red and held a strained expression.

"Hello again, you two," I greeted them, "Back so soon?"

The old boy smiled and lay a gentle hand on his wife's shoulder, " Oh yes," he said slightly breathless, "I have to bring her to see you at least once a month, otherwise she has an orgasm!"

I was genuinely stunned. To this day I can't believe he meant to say that to me, but I can't think of what other word he thought he was saying. I'm not even sure if he knew what an orgasm was. (Apparently, according to Rradio 4's Woman's Hour, they weren't invented until the 1960s)

He painted a wonderful mental image in my head. I could picture the old dear clutching the sides of her wheelchair and hanging on for dear life as she panted and groaned in ecstasy. "Ohh Cyril, quick, get me down the market. I'm having one of my turns again!"

It wasn't until later that I thought about what the man had said. According to him, a visit to me actually 'stopped' his wife from having an orgasm, not caused one. I freely admit that I am not the best looking man in the world. Dilly often tells me that if beauty is skin deep, then I'm inside out! But I did find the couple's accusation a trifle harsh. That didn't stop me putting my new found talent on my business card though.

After all, if you've got it, flaunt it!

NICK RICHARDSON
WATCHES, STRAPS, BATTERIES,
CLIMAXES NIPPED IN THE BUD (weekends only)
SPECIAL RATE FOR PENSIONERS

Chapter 9

COME FLY WITH ME

'The universe must not be narrowed down to the limit
of our understanding, but our understanding must be
stretched and enlarged to take in the image of the universe as
it is discovered.'

Francis Bacon.

I almost had an OBE recently. Although this wasn't a thank you from a grateful nation; I am talking about an Out of Body Experience. I had just had one too many glasses of wine, and I had risen from my chair only to discover that somebody had swapped my legs for those of a newborn calf. All four corners of the room started to move in different directions and I could feel my consciousness slipping away. I was at that strange midway point of reality, a weird nether-world only visited when drunk. I had just come out of the 'happy euphoric' stage, the stage that makes you think that you are actually good at Karaoke. A world where your eyes are able to look in two different directions at once, yet remain unable to focus on either of them.

This was, of course, a spiritual experience only in the sense that it was bought on by *too many* spirits, but it got me thinking about genuine out-of-body experiences, (OBEs)

- those times when people consciously slide out of their body and go astral travelling; I wish I could do it. I would secretly visit my neighbour's house and find out what he did with my hammer-drill and orbital sander.

Evidence of Out-of-Body Experiences, is noted throughout history. Across cultures, religions and languages, people have documented the separation and return of a spirit body or soul from the physical body. Writings in ancient Greece record OBEs through philosophers such as Plato and Herodotus, and even before this, Egyptian priests were aware of the existence of the astral body.

Mostly, OBEs happen unexpectedly, with the majority of them occurring when people are in bed, ill, or resting. It is also possible for an episode of exhaustion, anxiety or shock to cause the astral body to briefly separate from the physical body.

Recent experiments in OBEs, by researchers in Britain and Switzerland, used virtual reality goggles and cameras located behind volunteers to induce the feeling of viewing their body from somewhere outside of itself. The volunteers did indeed have the weird sensation of an OBE and therefore a lot of the national press were quick to point out that an OBE must be no more than a trick of the mind. However, this experiment does not explain other phenomena associated with real OBEs, such as viewing a previously unseen object beyond their range of vision – on a high shelf, for example, in the next room or even outside of the building, or hearing a conversation that is taking place a long way away from the person experiencing the OBE. These phenomena are also associated with Near Death Experiences (NDEs). These experiments certainly don't prove that OBE's are 'all in the mind.' In fact Bigna Lenggenhager, a psychologist with the Swiss Federal Institute of Technology, noted that the setup, while an extremely useful tool for testing the limits of self-perception, is only the beginning of better research on the brain, stating that, "We've shown the 'body' and 'self' is somehow separate in the brain, even though we didn't invoke a completely realistic [out-of-body experience],"

One very compelling case of an OBE happened to an American singer/songwriter called Pam Reynolds. She had a very complicated brain operation. As you can imagine this was a very closely monitored procedure, and you can't get much more 'scientific' than a state of the art operating theatre. So deep was her anaesthesia that she was clinically dead, with no blood flowing to her brain and a monitor indicated that she had no brain wave activity at all. During the operation she claims that she was pulled out of her body and floated above herself. She remembers being curious about the drill that the surgeon was using as she thought it resembled an electric toothbrush, which struck her as odd as this was not what she imagined they would use to cut open her skull. She also remembered a conversation between the nurse and the surgeon regarding how small her arteries were. She then claims she was taken into a white light where she met loved ones who had passed to spirit. She made a full recovery from her operation, and doctors were amazed when she gave them a comprehensive rundown of the procedure she had received. The medical staff confirmed that she was correct in every detail, even down to the tools used in the operation. The nurse also corroborated that she and the surgeon had indeed discussed the issue of her arteries. So comprehensive and detailed was the information she gave, that there was only one positive explanation; a part of her consciousness had observed the operation.

The only time I can say with any truthfulness that I have myself had an OBE was when I was a child. However, back then I wasn't quite sure what was happening and wondered if I was dreaming. It is only looking back as an adult that I realise I can recall every single moment as if it were yesterday, and observe that the feelings I had were **very** different to dreaming.

My experiences were always the same; I would float out of my body and leave it sleeping in the bed. I can remember gliding towards the ceiling and looking back at myself, observing how much easier it was to move about without the constraints of gravity. Next, I would float silently down the stairs and look around the doorway into the living room, where my mother, father and sister would be sitting having supper. At this point I would try and speak. 'Hey, look at me, aren't I clever? I can fly.' I wanted to say. They would have been so impressed; especially as they were always telling me I wouldn't amount to much. How proud they would have been to have a self-levitating son. It would have been so useful for cleaning the upstairs windows. However, just as I opened my mouth to speak I would feel a strong pulling from behind, dragging me backwards up the stairs. I'd grasp tightly on to the doorframe hoping to avoid being drawn back, but it was always to no avail. Some people report being connected to their body during astral travel via a golden cord or silver thread. Mine was more like a bungee rope, as it would pull me back into my body with a violent thwack. This part was always a bit strange and not always comfortable. I had absolutely no idea what caused these bizarre trips, if anything. I had no control over the situation and would always think 'oh no, here we go again' as I felt the inevitable tug of my consciousness being pulled from my body. Was there a 'trigger', I wondered? I was addicted to Tizer and Jelly Tots, a dangerous combination at the best of times, but I don't think they had anything to do with it. They always appeared to happen at random with no rhyme or reason behind them and at one point became more frequent than I was comfortable with. But why me? I'd never asked to be Peter-Pan.

I admit the 1970s was an odd decade, but I don't believe there was any social stimulus for my trips either, even though this was the decade of The Clangers and The Magic Roundabout, two of the most 'tripped out' TV shows ever.

I expect a number of people will claim that it was my brains response to dealing with some deeply buried emotional turmoil. I would roundly reject these claims of course. I had no childhood trauma other than Mr Cactypusscat. They might even surmise that it was the result of an over-active imagination. But why would I invent such a bizarre happening just to spice up my life a bit? *Believe me, my life was odd enough as it was.* Allow me to explain:

Money was tight in our household, and so were my shoes. For years my dear old dad worked two jobs. He had his main career as a printer, but he also took on any number of other tasks just so we could afford a holiday each year. One of his more unusual exploits involved him going around the local farms and collecting their empty animal feed- bags, which he then sold on to paper mills. This famously became known as 'Pig-bagging'. He stored them in the garage directly below my box room, and would wait until it was full to bursting before moving them on. You can only imagine the terrible stench of hundreds of old 'pig poo' covered feed bags. It's no wonder Nipper the Hamster made a desperate bid for freedom! Throughout the summer months my bedroom became the hottest spot in town for every Bluebottle within a ten-mile radius. My room was so small that when there were more than five flies in it there was no room for me.

As for my O.B.Es being a psychosomatic symptom of a disturbed childhood - reaching out to my family and being rejected- I can roundly deny these accusations. My parents positively encouraged me to take part in family life and invented a new game specifically for me to play; it was called 'Rinse My Pants.' Every Saturday, it was my job to lug a week's worth of the family's dirty washing to the local laundrette. This necessitated walking through our local estate, which could be an intimidating place at the best of times, but to do so whilst carrying a red plastic washing basket that showed your mothers and sisters knickers to the world was truly frightening. A swim through shark-infested waters with five kilos of rotten haddock down my trunks would have been less scary. To make matters worse, the laundrette was opposite the local playing fields.

For hours on end I would sit and watch my friends play football. They would invite me out for a game, even though I was crap, but I knew I wasn't to leave my post. My father had spelled it out to me plainly, "Son," he said earnestly, with one hand placed trustingly on my shoulder, "Never, ever leave the washing alone, and don't let it out of your sight for one minute, or else it will be gone. You know what they're like round here, they'll nick anything." He never fully explained who *they* were, after all, *they* were just other families exactly the same as ours. He would always finish with the same words, "Do not, I repeat, do not lose my vests!"

And so there I would sit, hour after boring hour, watching the washing spin around. Now and again my fathers paisley Y-fronts would appear at the glass and leer at me from amidst the foam and scum, they'd toss around for a couple of minutes and then disappear. The frightful colours were enough to bring on a psychedelic hallucination, and I often wondered if this was a contributing factor to my nightly flights of fancy. A strange sort of 'hypnotic trigger,' if you like. Those pants haunted my dreams for years, and believing as I do in reincarnation, I'm sure they've come back as my neighbour's tabby cat.

It wasn't all bad though, this crappy job did have its bonuses. For a start, the laundrette was always warm. I also became friendly with the other 'Saturday washers.' These were always old ladies who all looked the same, small hunched-over women wearing bright floral tabards, headscarves and furry carpet slippers. The cigarette of choice of this strange tribe was *Silk-Cut*.

Over the years I got to know them all pretty well, and these mother hens took me under their wings. I would like to think I became like a surrogate son to many of them. They'd offer me sweets, and on a few occasions, cigarettes, "You go out and play with your mates, son, we'll look after your washing," they'd offer kindly, and oh, it was so tempting, but my dad's voice would always ring alarm bells in my head. "Nick, take care of my vests." I'm sure they were lovely old dears, but what if it was just a cover? What if they really only hung around in these kinds of places hoping to steal other people's underwear? I could imagine them spiriting my father's pants away with them, back to their lonely houses. Perhaps their husbands had died years ago, and their lives had never felt complete since without a big pair of Y-fronts drip-drying over the kitchen sink. They might even sit the pants in an armchair at night and talk to them as if there was still a man in them. Perhaps discussing the state of Val Doonicans jumpers over double egg and chips? They might leave them strewn untidily around the house and then use this as an excuse to moan at them, "I'm forever cleaning up after you Harry, you dirty sod, I pity your poor mother, bringing you up."

No, it was too great a risk. I would have to sit there and act as sentinel over the family smalls.

Very occasionally, I broke this golden rule of guardianship and briefly relinquished my post. This would happen on the odd occasion that I found money in the coin-return tray of the washing machines. This became a lucrative pastime, but you had to make sure you got there before anyone else. I was lucky in the respect that I knew the place intimately. I knew who went in and out and at what time. I knew which old dears were absent-minded enough to not check for coins themselves. I also knew the secret nooks and crannies where dropped coins would roll into, inaccessible places to adult fingers but not to a skinny malnourished ragamuffin like me. I always made sure that at the bottom of the washing basket I had secreted a wire coat hanger, which was used, with some success, to explore the darker and dustier recesses under the machines. My resolve was often rewarded, and the fluff-covered treasure I found would be quickly hidden inside the pocket of my denim flairs, where it would burn a hole in my pocket, until I could stand the tension no longer and desert my post, leaving the washing forgotten and unguarded as I ran to the shop next door to buy a Texan Bar and a Toffee Log.

The other bonus from sitting in the laundrette was the smell of the dry-cleaning machine. This had a hard, 'varnish/petrol' chemically enhanced smell. Mother had always warned me not to sniff glue or felt-tip pens, but she never said anything about dry-cleaning machines. It was heaven, and worth putting 10p into the empty machine and letting the vapours fill the room.

There then came a dark episode in my life that made me wish with all my heart that I could call upon an OBE at will. It was an incident so shocking that those of a nervous disposition would do well to read no further.

I hated school with a passion. From the age of 5, until I left school at 16 my opinion never changed. I always found it a gross infringement of my liberties that I *had* to go, and that there was no option. You attended school – full stop! I didn't see it this way of course. As far as I was concerned, I was a free person. My poor mother fought a running battle with me every day to try and get me through the school gates. As the impending imprisonment approached ever nearer I would go to pieces. Come the time to say goodbye I was a hysterical wreck, clinging onto my mother's legs and pleading with her not to send me to my doom. I would kick, scream and shout in the way only a petulant child knows how. This routine happened every day for years.

On one occasion my junior school headmaster, Mr Preston, tried to intervene during one of my panic attacks and attempted to physically drag me into school, for which he received a smart kick on the shins from me for his trouble. He hopped around the playground clutching his leg and going red in the face, giving me my chance for escape, and I leapt at it. Mind you, my swipe at Mr Preston was no more than he deserved, and I considered it payback for the time he had confiscated Bernard, my Action Man with gripping hands and realistic scar. In my book, he got everything he deserved.

Having escaped his clutches I ran straight out of the school gates and made a dash for freedom. Unfortunately, my mother spotted me and gave chase, ending my bid for liberty by rugby-tackling me to the floor. My embarrassing behaviour was noted by my mother and before turning me in, the rotten grass, she said, "Just you wait till you get home," with as much menace as she could muster. I wasn't worried though; ultimately she was a soft touch and a bit of contriteness on my part and a light sprinkling of 'little boy charm' would soon calm the waters. But, dear reader, I never had chance to plead my case, for as soon as I set foot through the door that evening, she pounced on me like a feral cat on a mouse. Within a flash she grabbed me by the scruff of the neck, whipped her slipper off and waved it threateningly above her head. "What on earth was all that fuss about this morning?" she demanded. I still wasn't unduly worried by her hostile manner; after all, she had no previous history of child abuse. She was bluffing – I knew it and she knew it.

My downfall came, though, with my disrespectful, smug and conceited conduct. I turned my backside towards her with a swaggering 'you can't hurt me' kind of gesture and wobbled by bottom at her. "Ner, ner, ner, ner, ner." I sang cockily. Even the most saintly of human beings have a breaking point, and I had just discovered my mother's. I believe that at this point even the Dali Lama himself would have reached for the nearest weapon.

The smacks rang out around the house. I was so stunned that I forgot to cry. My mother was actually hitting me; my mother didn't do things like this. My brain couldn't actually process this information. It didn't recognise the signals that the nerve endings in my buttocks were sending it. My mother was the least aggressive person in the world, and this was like getting a vicious kicking from Mother Theresa. My sister heard the commotion and managed to tear herself away from *Magpie* on the television in order to come and witness this display of wanton aggression. She had a perverse look of glee on her face and her smile widened with every whack. If ever there was a time when I wanted an OBE, it was now. If only I had mastered the art of astral travel I would have slipped silently out of my body at that very moment and poured scorn down onto my mother and sister from my unique advantage point of the ceiling. Needless to say this didn't happen, and there is one good reason for that; **I couldn't command them at will, and I had no control over when they would strike.** They just happened randomly. And I can state categorically that they were not figments of my imagination made up to make my life more exciting, they were 'real' events. Whenever they happened I was always fully aware of my body being soundly asleep in the bed, but also fully aware that I was floating above it; both feelings were as 'real' as each other.

Although I make light of these incidents now and can have a bit of fun with them, I must admit that at the time they were truly frightening. It sometimes felt as if I was being 'stolen' out of my body! I also didn't know why they were happening, and they left me confused and unsure as to who I was. There was also the added worry of what would happen if I didn't make it back into my body. Would I die or just spend eternity floating around the nether regions of the Universe? I was okay during the daytime, but come the evening I would start to feel apprehensive. At one point I became scared of going to sleep in case 'they' came to get me. I say 'they' because it always felt as if some outside influence was at work.

Now at this point you are probably wondering why I have 'aired my dirty laundry in public, so to speak, and what on earth does all this have to do with my dad's pants and the laundrette? Well, sitting in that laundrette for hours on end gave me time to think. Although I used to make a fuss about doing the laundry, in reality I was glad to get out of the house and I needed something that was the complete opposite to an OBE. I needed normality, and being surrounded by 'ordinary' people helped to ground me. In some respects the time I spent in the laundrette could be termed an In Body Experience. What on earth was happening to me at nighttime? Did this happen to anyone else? I didn't dare ask my friends, who all thought I was weird enough as it was without telling them that I floated around the house at night. Talking to old ladies or watching my friends play football felt normal and was the antithesis to everything that I was experiencing at night. As daft as it sounds, that laundrette became a safe haven for me. It allowed me some respite from the trauma of nighttime. Thankfully these episodes only lasted a few more months and then faded away. I wasn't sorry when they stopped.

I was too young to realise it at the time, but these OBEs were actually an important milestone on my journey of discovery, because what they did offer me was a glimpse into a multi-dimensional world. They actually served as proof as to the multi-faceted nature of consciousness. It showed me how we are so much more than just a collection of skin and bones. We have our 'real' wide-awake selves, but we also have another self that is able to externalise its consciousness outside of the body. Research has shown that 1 in 10 people claim to have had an OBE at some point in their lives. Anyway, if the soul comes in to the body at birth and then leaves again at death, why should we think it strange that it has the ability to pop in and out when it feels the need to? As the soul is *separate* from our body, it's not unusual for the soul to travel *externally* from it. After all, our earthly body is something that our spirit finds useful: a tool to carry our consciousness.

On a recent trip back I went past that old launderette, it is now a chip shop—frying tonight anyone?

***

I decided recently that it would be a wise move to subject my business to a comprehensive and wide-ranging overview of its security and crime-prevention requirements. In these days of 24 hour CC TV and our seemingly ever-increasing security conscious world, I decided it was high time that I had a look at my options for theft prevention. After all, you can never be too careful. After a comprehensive risk assessment, and a monetary review of any cost implications, I came up with a cunning plan. I felt it was a solution that was both technologically sound and financially viable, so, after careful scrutiny and due consideration, I implemented this high tech security scheme... and installed a doorbell.

The risk of theft isn't an issue that I lose much sleep over. The occasional problem arises (more on that later!) but generally the only crime in Cornwall – apart from exorbitant car parking fees – is the risk of being mugged for your ice cream by a passing herring gull. These airborne Mafioso have honed and developed their assault tactics to a fine art. They can swoop down to within inches of your face and be off with your snack before you have even noticed it has gone.

One of my watch display cabinets has sliding doors, which enables customers to help themselves. I had a cheap and tacky doorbell given to me and decided that it might provide some fun and light relief if I was to install this particular cabinet with a false alarm system. I fastened the bell push to the underside of my counter and subsequently hid the speaker unit out of sight on top of the display cabinet. As customers slid the glass doors open I would surreptitiously press the bell-push and take great satisfaction in watching old ladies jump and recoil in shock as they think they have activated a warning system. It's amazing how high some people can leap when they are suddenly confronted with such intimidating tunes as Roll Out The Barrel' or 'I Dream Of Jeannie' blaring out next to their ears. As you can see, this is a particularly classy piece of electronic wizardry. At my fingertips I have the choice of up to fifty different tunes – all of them terrible, hardly recognisable as music and each one sounding as if it was being played by a child of four on a Rolf Harris stylophone.

A lady recently enquired of me if I had a replacement battery for a cordless doorbell.

"Have you brought the remote bell pusher with you?" I asked her.

"No, I've left it at home; I've only brought the old battery with me." she replied. She placed it on the counter in front of me. It was a silver disc about the size of a 10 pence coin.

I instantly saw the opportunity for some fun. I found the new battery she required and placed it, still in its transparent packaging, next to the old one on the counter.

"Just press the old battery and see if there's any life left in it." *I suggested. She placed her finger on the battery and pushed. I cupped my hand around my ear as if straining to hear a distant sound.*

"I can't hear anything," I said, "Yes, that old battery is definitely dead." *I pointed to my fresh replacement. "Right, now try pressing the new one," I encourage her. She did as she was instructed and pushed down on the new battery. Once again I gave the impression of listening to a distant sound. "No, I don't think you pressed it hard enough. Try again." Once more she pushed down hard, only this time leaning over slightly to add more weight to her efforts. "No – still no good." I said. "Try using your other hand." She did so; meanwhile, my spare hand found my own secret bell push and pressed it simultaneously. The melodic strains of 'Colonel Bogie' suddenly filled the air. I gave a triumphant smile. "There you go!" I chirruped, "You were using the wrong hand. You've got a left handed doorbell."*

A look of horror crossed her face, "But I'm right handed," she cried.

"Not to worry," I said, "You never ring your own doorbell, but you will need to warn all your friends."

"Oh I will, she replied, "As soon as I get home, I'll phone them all and tell them, and just to be safe I'll put a note on the door."

***

Chapter 10

GRAND DESIGNS

'If you are in a spaceship travelling at the speed of light
and you turn on
your headlights, does anything happen?'
Steven Wright

The Cornish farmer leaned in towards me until his red nose was only inches away from mine. His breath had the faint aroma of turnips.

"Get your tent out of my field before I fill your backside full of lead!"

I heeded this sound advice and was gone in a flash. I wasn't doing any harm, but I had obviously offended the old chap by setting up camp in what was effectively his back garden. Cornish farmers have a fearsome reputation that is, in some cases, richly deserved. I wasn't prepared to stand and argue with a man who cradled a twelve-bore shotgun in his arms as if it was a newborn babe. My feeble attempts at an apology just made him furrow his brow until his forehead was as rutted and wrinkled as one of his ploughed fields. I hastily packed my belongings into my rucksack and made a swift exit, all the while staring over my shoulder to make sure that no buckshot was about to become intimate with my derriere. This had happened twenty years ago, but the moral had stuck with me: Always ask before entering onto farmland.

In the summer of 2004, I once again found myself conversing with a farmer, this time in Wiltshire. I was asking if he would mind us taking a closer look at the crop circle that had appeared in his field during the night.

"Yeah, no problem!" he said, "Just try and stick to the side of the field if you can. Oh, and by the way, that'll be £2 each, thank you." This had become an annual trip for my wife and I. It's a part of the country that we adore, and we had managed to slip away for a few days of rest, relaxation and crop circle hunting.

The term 'circle' is slightly misleading for these elegant and complex creations. The unique and increasingly intricate designs appear overnight – apparently being created in minutes. They aren't a new phenomenon however, as reports of these strange occurrences go back hundreds of years, but in recent times they certainly appear to be getting more and more complex with each year that passes. Genuine circles are often complex mathematical and geometric shapes, the likes of which are normally only seen on the Open University, drawn on blackboards by mullet haired men in dodgy tank-tops. But how do the designs get there? Are they all a huge hoax? Are they UFO landing sights? (Is it me, or do most UFO's resemble Jaffa cakes?) Or are they the flamboyant result of farmers getting in touch with their artistic sides and being creative with a Flymo? Or could they perhaps be messages from another realm of consciousness? On this trip we had two days to find out. We were certainly in the right place. Southern England is responsible for ninety percent of the world's crop circles, with the vast majority of these occurring in Wiltshire.

The shape we approached through the wheat was soon nicknamed 'The Bee,' because of its insect like appearance. Once inside the circle we managed to gain some perspective on its huge size. It was approximately 91 metres long, which is just over 289 feet – or the length of an American football field.

This was surely no hoax. The grain was swirled into complex patterns and you could almost trace the vortex of power that had created this design. The stalks were laid over one another in great swathes, as though a strong wind had pushed them down one way and then quickly changed direction and pressed in another way. The whole image was as if the stalks had been woven together, in a similar way to how cane furniture knits together to create its distinctive shapes.

Interestingly, few of the stalks were broken. Most were bent at 45 degrees about 2 inches above the ground. The bend in the stalk always appears on a joint or nodule, causing a large swelling. It is well documented that in genuine circles the crop will eventually re-grow, showing little sign of damage. This is of course untrue for hoaxed circles. These are normally formed by people flattening the crop with scaffold boards or wide planks of wood. This snaps the stems at soil level and kills the crop completely.

From ground level it is difficult to appreciate the true beauty of these creations; the best view is from the air. Frantically patting my pockets, I realised I had left my 35ft inflatable step ladders at home, but not to worry, as aerial photos are usually published on the web within hours. It is interesting to note that genuine circles provide evidence that is missing in hoaxed ones. In a genuine circle it is frequently reported that electrical and mechanical apparatus doesn't work. Mobile phones that refuse to work inside the circle can be held at arms length outside the circle and are suddenly be found to be working. This anomaly can be found around the whole perimeter of the design. High levels of electro- magnetic energy can be found in the genuine display that is missing in the hoax. Probably the biggest difference between the genuine and the hoax is the condition of the crop itself. The Canola oil plant is very brittle. When it is bent beyond 45 degrees it snaps clean off. When genuine crop circles have been found in Canola, the stalks are bent at 90 degrees. Scientific analysis suggests that the only way to achieve this is by microwave or ultrasound influence. Biologists are at a loss as to how this occurs. Hoaxers can't re-create this phenomenon. Scientific research has also shown that the crystalline structure of plants from genuine circles is different to that of ordinary plants; molecular anomalies also appear in true circles. Seed heads were examined and found to be severely changed, often stunted or malformed in juvenile crops. As we had seen for ourselves, the nodules of stalks are swollen and sometimes appear to have burst open. This is explained by the rapid expansion of liquid within the stalk, due to a sudden and extremely virulent heat-source, similar to the force created by a microwave. As well as physical changes to the crop, you soon become aware of an atmospheric change held within the confines of a circle. It *feels* different inside the crop-circle to outside. It's hard to pinpoint exactly how the difference can be measured – perhaps it's an electromagnetic difference that occurs, that is picked up as subtle messages by one's own body.

As we walked around we noticed a palpable feeling of energy, a buzzing in the ears and a vibration through the hands. We sat quietly in the circle for a long time, absorbing the atmosphere. Although it had appeared by a busy road, we had the place to ourselves for over thirty minutes before we were eventually joined by another group of people who seemed as enthralled as we were by its splendour.

In his book *Secrets in the Fields*, Freddy Silva tells us that, in 1996 a 'circle' appeared in broad daylight next to Stonehenge without anyone witnessing its creation. A pilot and doctor had flown over the ancient site one July afternoon. They had a clear view over the stones below and nothing unusual was apparent. Forty five minutes later, after landing, the doctor was attempting to drive back past Stonehenge when he was caught up in a huge traffic jam. People had left their cars to look at a brand new crop circle within metres of the sacred stones. It was a sophisticated mathematical spiral of 149 circles. The "Julia Set" measured an immense 920 feet down its spine. That is 280 metres long.

The designs are frequently aligned with prehistoric sites, such as Avebury stone circle, Silbury Hill, or ancient barrows and earth mounds. This one lined up with one of Wiltshire's famous White Horses.

The next day we rose early and telephoned the 'crop circle help line,' which gives times and grid references to any new circles. A recorded message informed us of two new designs. Within twenty minutes I had dressed, shaved and sprinted my way through three bowls of shreddies. I sat in the car, waiting patiently for my wife, I had the engine running and I was raring to go. I sat for 10 minutes, raring to go. I rearranged the dust on the dashboard with an old cloth, raring to go. I watched the wiper blades scrape the corpses of a thousand flies from my windscreen, raring to go. I fiddled with the radio tuner, but could still only pick up French stations that were so clear you would think they were being broadcast from the boot – and, I was still raring to go. I yawned so violently that I nearly dislocated my jaw, but I was still raring to go. I fell asleep with my head resting against the seat belt and my tongue hanging limply over my drooping chin; my wife suddenly opened the door and sat down heavily making the car shake violently,

"Come on you lazy sod," she barked," I thought you were raring to go."

After a few choice words, and a couple of impressive wheel spins, we sped off with a sense of heightened anticipation to search for the first of the two circles.

We located the field and could already see people making their way along a track towards the new circle. We sprinted towards the design, but on entering, something didn't feel right. There were no swirls of corn, no swollen nodes and no clean edges to the design and the atmosphere inside felt completely flat. It's hard to describe an atmosphere; those hidden and unseen signs that we subconsciously pick up on. You can sometimes walk into an empty house and know instantly if it's a happy or sad place from the 'feeling' pervading the atmosphere. It's much the same with crop circles. This one was a hoax! The crop looked like a drunk had pushed a pram full of bricks around it and then hopped about with a dustbin-lid tied to his feet for good measure. The crop was universally snapped at ground level. You can fully understand any farmer being furious at such wanton destruction, with absolutely no hope of his crop re-growing.

A lady sat in the centre of the circle with a singing-bowl. She was making the bowl hum at a certain pitch. She sat cross-legged, eyes closed with her face pointing to the heavens, looking for all the world as if she was sending a telepathic message to be beamed up. I turned to my wife and whispered in her ear, "It's life Jim, but not as we know it."

We left feeling disappointed. However, I think it's important to approach each new circle with a completely open mind. You have to guard against convincing yourself that what you are looking at is genuine, just because you would like it to be so. Fake circles are always a good yardstick to measure genuine circles by.

We consulted the map again and soon found the location of the second circle. As luck would have it, it was only 200metres from a famous 'croppies' pub. The Barge Inn sits on the banks of the Kennet and Avon Canal, and has become a mecca for circle watchers everywhere. The walls of one of the bars are festooned with newspaper cuttings and aerial photographs of crop circles. At any time of day or night there always seems to be at least one person propping up the bar who can give you chapter and verse on the history of crop circles. I looked around for *Fox Mulder*, but he was nowhere to be seen. And, by the way, the Barge Inn does the best cauliflower cheese I have ever tasted.

The new circle was situated in a field adjacent to the pub, but on the opposite side of the canal. We had to walk miles down the towpath before we found a bridge that allowed us access to the other side. We then walked all the way back to opposite where we had started from. Oh, if only I could walk on water. The trek was well worth it though, as this temple in the corn was no hoax. It contained all the visual evidence of a large energy having moved and shaped the corn into incredibly intricate patterns without any damage. There was a palpable feeling of force, intelligence and willpower behind the image; a true sense of purpose to it.

So how do they get there and what exactly are they for? Well, let me have a stab at explaining it for you; I think they are sort of err, well, they are a bit like, stuff, you know that whizzes around a bit and well it, hmmm. (I've just realised that I sound like my father when I asked him what happens when you die. They do say you turn into your parents.) Perhaps I will let *Secrets in the Fields* author and world renowned expert Freddy Silva explain:

"Crop circles are expressions of living energy, a form of electro-magnetic and sonic energy with components of magnetism and anti-gravitational aspects.

When this energy hits a solid area, like a wheat field, the expression of that energy, its resonance, will actually create a geometric shape. Just as what happens when you send a sound frequency through a liquid, and you capture that sound frequency in a photograph.

It's a living energy field, encoded with information, which interacts with the earth on a physical level and expresses itself geometrically in harmonically pleasing patterns. There is a concise source behind this."

On the tip of my tongue...

That explanation puts paid to one of the more outlandish suggestions that was once offered; that they were the mating tracks of badgers! Lets face it, badgers aren't that clever. Have you ever seen one driving a bus or working in a chemist? Although,in 2009 BBC news reported some strange happenings in Tasmania. According to the Attorney General, wallabies were eating the crops of legally grown opium poppies on the island. Apparently, they ate so much that they became 'high' and then hopped around in circles, flattening the crop as they went leaving the appearance of having had a 'visitation'.

***

Wiltshire is a fascinating part of the world. In 2003, half the crop circles in the UK were within nine miles of Avebury. Avebury Stone circle and Silbury Hill draw me to them like a magnet. Every time we revisit and walk amongst the stones, it's like visiting old friends. The world seems to move around them, always busy and bustling, yet they seem impervious to change, standing still for millennia in a part of space and time that is strictly their own.

At nighttime the stones take on an unworldly air. The huge shapes loom out of the darkness and tower over you like immoveable giants, and yet I never feel scared or uneasy in their presence in the all-enveloping blackness. They have a protective quality to them; guardians and sentinels awaiting their time to awaken. On one night time sojourn, we took many photographs around the stones and on viewing the pictures later, discovered them to reveal hundreds of orbs clustered around the stones, overlapping each other and shining brightly against the night sky, as if a thousand stars had fallen to earth and danced around them.

The day after our crop circle encounter we walked around the Avebury stone circle for most of the day. At one point I had walked to a quiet corner of the field and sat with my back to a small outlaying stone. I closed my eyes and enjoyed the feeling of the sun on my face. My peaceful revelry was soon spoiled by a loud and raucous noise coming from the next field. Screams and excited yells were carried on the wind. I stood up to see what was happening and spotted a group of around 20 youths frolicking boisterously amongst the monoliths. Their accents gave them away as Americans. They carried clipboards and were obviously students on a field trip. They seemed oblivious to the disruption they were causing as they barged past anybody who happened to be in their way, showing a flagrant disregard for the sanctity of this world heritage site. Before long they entered the field I was in. Two huge stones act as a gate way to this field, each of them reaching fully 12 feet into the sky. Two students clad in baseball caps, (on backwards) decided that these two mountainous peaks needed conquering and scrambled haphazardly to the top of them. They proceeded to stand and shout from their vantage point and douse their friends with Coca Cola from a bottle they were waving. Their fellow students were obviously impressed with their bravado and stood 'hootin' an' a hollerin'' in encouragement.

"Yo, Randy, take a picture of me an' Bubba." One of them yelled from the summit.

There are signs all around the Avebury complex ordering you not to climb on the stones. But of course the signs are written in English and not American, which is why these students couldn't understand them. I think they must have thought the term 'World Heritage Site' was Olde Worlde English for theme park.

Bubba and Chuck continued their juvenile display atop the rocks, waving their arms and whooping loudly. I was incensed. Did they treat other ancient sites in this way?

Would they go into St Paul's Cathedral and wash their feet in the font? Play a game of baseball amongst Stonehenge? Probably not, but I was angered by their Spiderman routine.

"Get off the stones!" I called crossly in my best PE teacher's voice. They were about 50 yards away and consequently didn't hear me. I took a deep breath.

"GET OFF THE BLOODY STONES YOU MORONS..!" I yelled through cupped hands. They heard that! They all turned to look at me. I frantically waved my arms gesturing in no uncertain terms for them to dismount. The two primates clambered down in an ungainly fashion. I wondered weather Zoology rather than Archaeology might have been a more suitable subject for them to study. Their lack of respect for such a magical and precious place left me feeling nauseous. Little did they know that energy centres like this one are closely guarded by Elementals from un-seen dimensions, (and we aren't talking about Mr Cactypusscat here.) These are **serious** places. As the group walked past me, one of the girls threw me a pitiful glance and muttered under her breath in a smug nasal whine, 'Gee, sorry,' in a tone that meant, 'Get a life you old git.' She was wearing a MacDonald's baseball cap...

Avebury village and its enclosing stone circle stand on the famous Michael Line. This is a principle leyline that runs through St Michael's Mount in Cornwall, Glastonbury and Avebury. At Beltane – otherwise known as May Day –

the sun rises directly along this line. So if you watched the sunrise from on top of St Michael's Mount, it will also be rising directly over Glastonbury and Avebury. The enduring legacy of the largest Stone Circle complex on Earth is that we still don't know why it was built. Its size and complexity make it obvious that it was of supreme importance to the people who built it. The whole area is enclosed by a ditch which was originally 64 feet wide and 36 feet deep.

It makes you marvel at how they excavated this land with nothing more than a few deer antlers for tools. It's hard to comprehend the amount of man-hours this must have entailed. There were originally ninety-eight Sarcen stones, some weighing in at over forty tons. During recent investigations on the sight, one huge stone, buried seven feet under the earth, was estimated to weigh in at a colossal 100 tons. And to think I moaned like hell when I had to lay a new patio last year.

Silbury Hill lies about a mile distant form the stone circle. Although it stands beside a busy main road, the hill can still be reached via a footpath through fields. This is by far the best way to approach as it gives you some perspective as to how large it is. The hill is in your eye line at all times, but as you walk towards it, it appears to be getting further away. The nearer you get the more you appreciate how it dominates its landscape. Silbury Hill is the largest man-made mound in Europe (except for my next door neighbour's butt-cheeks that is!) It is thought to have been built at around the same time as the great pyramid at Giza.

I can still remember my first ever sighting of Silbury Hill. We came across it by accident at 1 o'clock in the morning, some eighteen years ago. Dilly and I had been to a funeral in Oxfordshire and were making our way back to Cornwall. It was over the Easter period, and as you can imagine, the roads were full to bursting. We had intended to use the motorway but on seeing the nose-to-tail traffic jams we decided to detour across country without a map. Before long we were hopelessly lost and following signs for any town that we vaguely recognised in the vain hope of finding our bearings from there. Our journey was further hampered by having a puncture and once Dilly had fixed this (I have very delicate hands) we were hopelessly behind schedule.

By the time we resumed our journey it was dark. After a while a mist began to hang over the roads, and as we drove slowly around a corner a huge shape loomed out of the fog as if it was barring our way. The car headlights seemed to be swallowed up by its vast bulk and gradually the cone shape of Silbury Hill revealed itself to us, leaning over us out of the darkness. All around us there were no signs of modern existence. There were no streetlights, and in contrast to the still busy motorways, this country road was deserted and the lights from any nearby farms were extinguished by the cloak of fog. It felt as if time had slipped and it was just us and the hill alone in the world. Was this a brief glimpse of how it was viewed by man all those thousands of years ago?

Silbury is mainly constructed of layers of gravel, soil and chalk. Although it is now covered in grass, it is thought that at one time it was a mound of luminous white chalk. This must have been an impressive site in Neolithic times. Oh, what wouldn't I give to time-travel? To spend just a few moments and peek into the lives of the people who used these sacred sites. To walk amongst them and discover how they lived. Did they look like me? Would I understand any of their language? Was it a hierarchical society, with upper and lower classes? Was this mound and stone circle used for some religious ceremony or were they a kind of calendar, helping Neolithic man to judge the seasons for crop planting and harvesting? It has been suggested that a large pole planted into the top of Silbury Hill would cast a shadow long enough to reach its base, and therefore act as some kind of clock or calendar – who knows? To me it seems an awful lot of work to go to just to make a bloody big watch. I think it's nice that we don't have a definitive answer to some of these questions. It retains their mystique and leaves them aloof and almost out-of-reach of our modern-day minds. All we can do is ponder on their reasons for existing

The hill is now out of bounds to the general public, as it was starting to wear away with the amount of people climbing it. It is easy enough to find a quiet spot in an adjacent field and to sit and gaze at this wondrous site. There have been times that I have felt what can only be described as a pulse emanating from Silbury Hill – a strange feeling that affects you in the solar plexus. It is almost as if this huge mound of earth in front of you is rhythmically vibrating.

I have always found it a special place. I can't quite put my finger on what its attraction is for me; after all it is just a mound of earth, although thousands of years ago it obviously held more significance than that. All I do know is that Silbury Hill exerts a hold over me that is not matched by anywhere else in the world that I know of. It seems to work on me at a level that surpasses my understanding. If I knew why it attracted me so much perhaps it would lose some of its mystery.

Top Tips

- Don't climb on the stones at Avebury
- When 'Cropping,' remember: always try and get permission to enter a field.
- If you can't get permission, wear armour-plated underwear.

***

He was around 15 years old, dressed smartly, well spoken and polite. It was a quiet day and we had spent some time discussing cricket, school holidays and such like, and he struck me as an intelligent and likeable chap. He was with a lady, whom I presumed to be his mother. She had wandered off to look elsewhere and he had offered to stay behind and look around my displays of watches. I busied myself with tidying up and restocking shelves. After a while I noticed that every time I caught his eye he quickly glanced away. This normally rings alarm bells in my head. I made a deliberate point to look at him every couple of minutes, and every time our eyes met, he quickly looked to the floor and shuffled his feet uncomfortably. I was astounded. 'He couldn't possibly...' I thought, 'Could he..?'

I have a large stockroom behind my counter, and once in there, I can't be seen, I can, however, see out. I stood only 18 inches in front of him – and he had absolutely no idea that I could see his every move. His behaviour became more agitated; he kept looking to a cabinet of watches that had obviously taken his eye and then quickly up to my sales counter, checking for me. Eventually, the prospect of a free watch got the better of him; he opened the cabinet in a flash and secreted one of the watches up the sleeve of his jacket. I couldn't believe it. He looked such an unlikely criminal. I mean, he was wearing a cardigan and had a side parting for goodness sake! I nonchalantly reappeared and stood behind my counter, acting as if nothing had happened.

"Everything okay mate..? Seen anything you want to buy?"

"Oh no, no, I'm fine, thank you very much." He played it cool, and pretended to look at a few more items, before saying, "Oh well, I must be going. Cheerio."

I gave a friendly wave and let him walk about 10 paces clear of my unit. At this point I expect he was just congratulating himself on his perfect execution of a faultless heist.

"Just a minute," I called after him, almost by way of an afterthought. "I think you've forgotten something..."

He turned and smiled, "No I don't think so." he said, patting his pockets.

"Are you sure?" I asked, walking towards him.

"Yes, perfectly sure thank you."

"Do you know what?" I said, "I'm certain you forgot to pay for that watch –the one you've hidden up your sleeve." He stood silent for a moment. I could almost hear his brain ticking over, trying to assimilate the information it was receiving.

"The one up your sleeve..?" I repeated, "Let me make it clearer for you – the one you're STEALING from me!" His eyes opened so wide he looked like a startled

prawn; I was speaking to him in such a kindly manner that I think he was having trouble believing that he'd been rumbled. He must have been so certain that he'd gotten away with it, and now he'd now been thrown into total confusion.

Very slowly, his look went from one of an angelic cherub to that of a newly condemned prisoner. He quickly reached for his wallet.,

"I've got the money, please take it, please." he begged. "Take more, whatever you need." His voice began to falter, no doubt caused by having to make its way past the rising panic stuck in his throat. I waved the wallet away.

"No way," I replied, "You had the chance to pay and you chose not to. Now it's my turn to choose. Let's see, do I call the police or not? You'd better come and stand behind my counter." I ordered, "We'll wait until your mother comes back before I decide what to do with you." He looked as if he was about to vomit.

"The lady I was with isn't my mother." he sobbed "She's my Aunty."

I faked a look of horror, "Oh, the shame of it." I said helpfully. "You amaze me, you had the money in your wallet all along, and yet you thought stealing was a better option. I've paid for all this stock and you're taking money directly out of my pocket." He went pale as I lifted down a photograph of my young sons. Two happy smiling faces dressed in school uniform beamed out from the picture. "Do you realise you are stealing food out of their mouths?"

I made him stand by my side as I served a few customers, explaining to each one as to why he looked like a rabbit caught in the headlights. All the old ladies were suitably shocked.

"Oh, he looks as if 'butter wouldn't melt!'" one of them said.

"You wanna' chop his hand off!" another offered helpfully.

His gaze never lifted from the floor and he looked more ashamed and wretched with every passing comment. Eventually, his aunty arrived and one look at the poor boy's face was enough for her to know that something was terribly wrong.

"Why Michael..." she said in a compassionate manner, "Whatever is the matter?" He could contain himself no longer and exploded loudly,

"OH GOD! STEALING, STEALING, I CAN'T BELIEVE IT, I'VE BEEN STEALING. WHAT WILL PEOPLE THINK OF ME?" he wailed forlornly, "OH NO, STEALING, STEALING!"

At this point 'Aunty' gave wonderful moral support by saying,

"Oh no, whatever will your mother say?" This set him off again on another round of breast-beating. I quickly

pulled a stool towards him and made him sit down, while he sobbed uncontrollably into his hands. 'Any minute now,' I thought, 'I'm going to have to put him in the recovery position.' I looked around for my first-aid kit, but all it contained was a second-hand bandage, two plasters and a cough drop.

I never expected such a reaction. I felt completely and utterly ashamed of myself for playing with this boy's emotions. Admittedly, he'd stolen from me, but hey, who am I to throw stones? In my defence, I had no reason to expect this display of total emotional collapse. I thought he might be slightly worried for ten minutes, we'd all agree he'd been a bit silly, and that would be an end to it. By the way I was feeling it would seem that the burden of guilt had engulfed me as well.

Once the boy had regained his composure, I told him that I thought he had obviously learnt a lesson and that I would take no further action in the matter. His Aunt agreed that it could be 'their little secret,' and that 'mummy will never know.' After a further five minutes of wiping his nose on his sleeve, he apologised and thanked me for not calling the police.

So, a case of, 'all's well, that ends well,' you might think. Well, not quite. About twenty minutes later it suddenly dawned on me, that at no point had he given me the stolen watch back, and at this moment it was now miles away and probably still safely hidden up the boy's sleeve.

***

Chapter 11

MIND OVER MATTER

'There are worse things in life than death.
Have you ever spent the evening with an insurance
salesman?'
Woody Allen

I'm very good at doing nothing. It's a skill I have perfected over many years of being a lazy sod. I can sit for hours in the garden quite happily without feeling the need to get up and do anything. Especially those pointless tasks, like cutting grass, or murdering weeds. When I sit on the beach I am more than happy to spend eons just watching the waves. I occasionally lift my hand to my face, so that I can lick an ice-cream or take a swig from a cold drink, but generally, the tide moves more in a day than I do.

You would therefore think that I would find it quite easy to meditate. To be able to sit quietly and disappear into my own little world – but for quite a while I found it tricky, as I seemed to lack the discipline it required. Every time I tried to 'drift off,' I kept getting the image of Robin Williams in my head. At the end of every episode of *Mork and Mindy*, he could be seen using meditative brain power to contact his guide and mentor. The screen would go all wobbly, and in a big reverberating voice he would call out,

'Mork calling Orson – come in Orson.' I could never shift this image. In truth, I think I struggled to take myself seriously.

I've always been jealous of people who find it easy to clear their head of thought and drift off into a trance-like state. They sit there oblivious to everything that happens around them, in calm serenity. I often wonder if they are really *that* deep, *that* detached. I'm always drawn to the idea of tickling their feet or jabbing them in the backside with a sharpened pencil. Surely they'd move then, wouldn't they? I know it's cruel, but I feel resentful. I've tried and tried but I can't seem to quieten my thoughts enough. My head won't empty of the chitchat that fills it. I've had a crack at all sorts of methods. I've tried thinking of just a single colour and repeating it again and again in my head like a mantra - 'red, red, red…' *(A little voice intrudes, singing) 'When the red, red robin comes bob, bob bobbing along'*

"NO, go away!" I groan.

So I settle down again and have another go - 'yellow, yellow, yellow…'

'Tie a yellow ribbon round the old oak tree.' Why is it the most *irritating* songs that stick in my mind?

Other methods I've struggled with include breathing exercises. My first attempt made me hyperventilate and emit some terrifying honks like an asthmatic goose. On the second attempt I developed one of those strange nasal whistles; every time I exhaled I tooted the first two bars of *London's Burning!* Next I played soothing music. Gentle and soporific melodies emanated from the soundtrack. An hour later I was jolted awake as the CD turned itself off. I'd been asleep for the duration of the music with my chin on my chest, dribbling down my shirtfront.

I need a sanctuary, a space to call my own where I can't be disturbed. Unfortunately, the only place like that in my house is the bathroom. It's the only room with a lock on the door. Luckily, however, I do have another place that fits the bill; it's a rocky plateau high above the Atlantic breakers on Cornwall's north coast. On a misty day you can just about see your boots, but on a clear day the vista is quite magnificent. The coastline stretches away for miles to both north and south and the eye is drawn to the horizon line where sea meets sky. It's here that I finally find peace inside myself, and this is where I go to become re-acquainted and uncover the parts of myself that get buried in the hurly-burly of everyday life. Here I realise I have five senses; I hear the pulse of waves over sand, the breath of wind on my face carrying the scent of salt, the feel of granite beneath my hands, ancient and immortal. The taste of the pasty I ate for lunch... Being in these natural elements is when I find it easiest to slip away. It's at these times when I accept the earth as a truly *living* organism that connects the whole of life to it. To be 'at one' with nature is to be 'at one' with *yourself.* If you have trouble *going within*, my advice is to *get outside* .It works for me, and sometimes throws up the most remarkable and unexpected encounters.

The hooded figure rushed at me. Within a split second he had closed the gap between us and his face was so close to mine that I couldn't focus properly on his features. He moved ever closer, until the whole of my vision was filled with the sight of his left eye, as he seemed to stare deep down into my soul. I fell backwards heavily, and landed with my feet in the air, like an upturned turtle.

"Dodgy pickled onion, darling?" Dilly asked casually.

I lay for a minute gazing up into the clear blue sky, slightly breathless.

"No, nothing to do with onions," I said, "Just a strange meditation."

We had chosen our picnic spot carefully, a small stone circle deep in the heart of the Cornish countryside. It was the middle of summer and a perfect day. Sunshine warmed our backs and a gentle breeze carried the scent of a nearby wild flower meadow. We sat in the tall grass and enjoyed the peace that solitude brings.

I had gorged myself happily on a mound of sandwiches that were three parts 'cheese' to one part 'flying insects.' Luckily, the aforementioned pickled onions had kept the larger winged predators at bay. They were afraid to travel too near to me, lest I breathe on them and incinerate them to oblivion – in a modern day re-enactment of the foolish Icarus and Dedalus.

It was such a peaceful place that I could feel the urge for a meditation coming on. Just a ten-minute *quickie* I thought. I sat cross-legged, relaxed, took a few deep breaths and tried to give the impression that I knew what I was doing.

Before long, I had drifted into that soporific state where time bears no relevance. The here and now began to fade away, the only interruption being the heavy drone of a passing bumblebee looking for all the world like a flying hamster. ("Nipper is that really you?") I was wandering happily down the back-roads of my subconscious mind, when I was rudely interrupted. A person marched into my field of vision from right to left. At this point I couldn't see his face, because it was cowled beneath a hood. The clothes he wore were loose fitting and appeared to be made of hessian, and were the colour of freshly dug clay. He wore britches that were bound around with leather cord from the knee downwards and heavily stitched ankle length boots. He had a quiver of arrows slung across his back and carried a bow in his left hand. He suddenly turned and looked directly at me, almost as if *I'd* startled him. Can you believe that? I startled him –this was my imagination not his! He had the look of a consummate hunter on the prowl, and he'd spotted me as prey. That was when he charged at me, invaded my space and stared deeply into my eye. You can now understand why I fell backwards. As we were near a stone circle, it did cross my mind that this chap might have been a sentinel or protector of the site. Ordinarily I would have passed this character off as a figment of my imagination, but two recent episodes had convinced me that things seen in meditation can sometimes be validated in the most remarkable of ways.

I had only recently interviewed the talented psychic artist Patrick Gamble for a magazine article. As part of the interview Patrick had offered to paint one of my Spirit Guides. He insisted beforehand that I tell him nothing about myself or my beliefs lest it influenced what he was to paint

As we chatted, Patrick's hands moved at manic speed across the canvas. His gaze was fixed about 3 feet above my head, and to my untrained eye, he seemed to be staring intently at empty space. He explained to me that the image he sees is like looking at somebody's face through water - as if the energy used to create the image moves in ripples. After about 20 minutes, Patrick's body seemed to relax and he sat back in his chair.

"All finished," he said, "are you ready?"

I was, I'd been looking forward to the session, but I had arrived with no pre-conceived ideas about what he might paint. As far as I was concerned a picture of Nipper would have been more than satisfactory.

He spun the canvas around, and there staring back at me was the face of a monk. I have to declare I was completely and utterly stunned.

"Oh my god, I know him, I know him!" I blurted out in an excited voice.

"I know you do." Patrick said confidently. "His name is Francis."

For years, whenever I went into a meditative state I would see a monk. I had learned to accept whatever images or thoughts came into my head without judgement. I would allow them to pass through my mind and saw them as random happenings, and never contemplated them too deeply. But this particular monk kept cropping up. In the end I became so used to seeing him that I hardly took much notice, until he started to make me laugh. If I was 'trying' too hard to meditate and not getting anywhere, he would frequently appear and start to yawn, or tap impatiently at an imaginary watch. On one memorable occasion when I was meditating late at night he walked through my eye line wearing a long nightshirt and winding a huge alarm clock. The images were so random that they made me laugh out loud. His message was obvious; *don't take yourself so seriously, relax and stop 'trying' so hard.* I always took his appearance at face value and accepted that my imagination had just created a funny and well-rounded figure, and I never thought of him as 'real'.

I sat staring at the picture. This was no passing resemblance. The hair colour was correct, so was the colour of his eyes, and his age was spot on at about twenty-five. The most remarkable fact was that in my meditations he had a slight droop to one side of his face, as if he had suffered from Palsy. Patrick's picture held a hint of this condition also. The more I looked, the more profound the experience became. I'd always had a belief in the afterlife, guides, reincarnation and such like, but no matter how many books you read or how much research you do, it's always nice to have proof. To me this was **solid proof**. At last, this was my *Road to Damascus* moment, and I was intensely moved by the experience.

How on earth, I wondered, could somebody I'd never met before, paint a picture of a person I'd only ever seen in my head? It doesn't serve as proof to anyone else of course. But it wasn't for anyone else – it was for me,

This was an incredibly productive time in my life, and a few weeks later a very similar thing happened again. I was doing a joint meditation with my friend Nancy. She is an accomplished healer and psychic, and we had got together for a catch up as to what was going on in our lives. We are never short of conversation, but on this day Nancy suggested that we do a meditation together. Mostly I tend to meditate on my own and so was happy to try a different approach. It worked very well because I found it easier than normal to drift away. Afterwards, we were chatting and Nancy revealed that she had seen some very clear images of something specific, and asked if I had seen anything of interest. This intrigued me, as I did have the very strong impression of a certain character, but I wasn't about to say who until Nancy had revealed what she had seen. "I saw a Native American Indian," she said with conviction, "However, he was dressed quite strangely. He was wearing a US cavalry jacket, buckskin trousers and a large and battered stove pipe hat!" Once again I was rendered speechless, for this was exactly the person I had seen. I love these kinds of happenings as they are so unexpected, and therefore all the more powerful.

There was no reason why I should have seen a Native American in my head. We hadn't discussed them beforehand, and although Nancy played music during our meditation, it was most definitely not the type of music that you would associate with American Indians. Even if the idea had been subconsciously planted in my head, its more likely that I would have imagined the archetypal image of an Indian, with a big headdress and war paint etc. So where did the cavalry jacket and battered hat come from? Why would we both see that? Once again I was left feeling dumbstruck that someone could see the exact image that was in my head.

On a personal level, meditation has enriched my life immeasurably. Soon after starting I began to find that I was a far calmer and measured person, and I became less intolerant and more patient of others. I acted on instinct and soon began to trust what I received through meditation as valid and worthy of my notice. It felt as if the clutter had been removed from my thinking and allowed my brain the room it needed to expand my perceptions. In the same way that sleep allows access to your subconscious mind, meditation throws open the doors to a different realm of consciousness.

Scientific research has shown that as well as psychological changes, meditating can also bring about physical changes to the brain itself. In a recent BBC documentary Dr Kathy Sykes looked into the subject of meditation and discovered that scientific experiments conducted by Sara Lazar of Harvard Medical School have shown that the cortex or outer layer of the brain is actually thicker on people who meditate on a regular basis than on those who don't. The physical structure of the brain has actually been changed by the process of meditation. It's easy to change a muscle structure in the body by exercising, but to be able to *think* a structural change is quite a different concept. The ever-advancing ability of brain imaging techniques are beginning to prove that meditation isn't 'all in the mind.' When people meditate, their brain waves change immediately. Scans have shown that during meditation certain areas of the brain remain quiet, whilst other areas that are normally quiet become active.

The brain is a mass of tiny nerve cells that communicate with each other by miniscule electrical impulses. These impulses can be detected by electrodes attached to the scalp as oscillations (more commonly known as brain waves.) They tend to fall into four different categories of frequency, called Beta, Alpha, Theta and Delta.

Beta Waves – 15-30 pulses (or waves) per second (Hz). You are probably in the "beta state" right now. This is the brain's tempo in a typical wakeful state linked with thoughts, deciphering problems, and full awareness directed towards the external world.

Alpha Waves – When you are really calm, your brain action slows from the quick tempo of beta, into the more serene waves of alpha – 9-14 Hz. Creative and inspired energy is activated, and you become more tranquil and feel a sense of peacefulness. Meditation can start in the alpha state and you can begin to access the store of creativeness, which is only just below the surface of our conscious awareness. Alpha is the opening into a deeper state of consciousness.

Deeper into meditation and stillness, you enter the **Theta state** – 4-8 Hz. This is where brain action slows nearly to the point of sleep. Whilst in the theta state you develop sharpened receptiveness, insight, and it is possible to remember distant and forgotten memories. It can often be the time that dream-like imagery flickers through your brain. It can often make you feel limitless and weightless. We experience theta only briefly as we awake from the deepness of sleep, or in the moments before going off to sleep. In theta, we may be open to information beyond our usual understanding. It is believed that 'theta meditation' stirs intuition and other sensitive or psychic abilities.

Brainwave activity has a tendency to echo flickering light, such as the light from an open fire, particularly when we are in the alpha and theta frequencies, as the flicker rate of fire happens to average in the alpha/theta range. This explains why we often slip into a peaceful or trancelike state while gazing into a fire. Although, I have to say, watching snooker on TV has me in a theta state within minutes.

Sound too has been shown to produce similar results. Pulsed rhythmic and binaural beats, (when one ear hears a clear tone of a slightly differing pitch than the other ear) can cause the brain to actually combine the discrepancy between the two beats and then keep pace with this pleasing, pulsing rhythm.

It is now possible to buy meditation machines. These combine sound and light frequencies and help the brain to achieve theta and alpha states. They are also a great way of cutting out the cost of expensive relaxation CDs, especially the one that has the sound of running water that has me sprinting for the loo in seconds flat. Hardly relaxing!

Delta Waves – 1-3 Hz. This is found during deep dreamless sleep and is the slowest brain-wave activity.

- The secret to effective meditation is relaxation. Remember not to exert any undue pressure on yourself. If you find it tricky at first, don't become frustrated, just stay focused.

- There is no right or wrong way to do it. What works for you is right for you. Have fun and experiment.

- Be patient. As with most things in life, I have found that the more I practise, the better I get, with the notable exception of golf!

The portrait of Francis now hangs on the wall alongside an assortment of grannies and granddads; most definitely one of the family. Some habits last a lifetime...

***

It was the end of a busy day and Jack had followed me out to my car. He had spent the majority of the afternoon regaling me with tales of his exploits. As we chatted his eyes fell upon something shining on my front seat.

"What's that?" he asked pointing.

"That's my new Harmonica." I said.

I had purchased it with the vague intention of becoming a second Springsteen or Neil Young, or if not a second, then at the very least a fourth or fifth. I reached in and handed it to Jack. He turned it over and over in his hands inspecting it minutely. He smiled.

"That's quite a good one that!" he exclaimed.

As daft as it sounds, I felt quite proud that he had endorsed it. Jack would have been the first to comment had I bought an inferior one. He then spent ten minutes giving me chapter and verse on the history of the harmonica. Strangely, he didn't claim to have invented it.

Within seconds, and to my horror, he raised it to his mouth, licked his lips and started to play! His cheeks puffed in and out like a pair of old bellows, whilst his eyebrows danced a jig along his forehead with every luxurious suck and blow. Of course the playing was pitch perfect, tuneful and melodic, but I am afraid it was lost on me, as all I could think of was the bacterial warzone that was Jack's mouth, and how this was now all being transferred into my harmonica. After ten excruciating minutes he stopped and smiled.

"Could you tell what it was?" he asked like a small boy.

"Was it Schubert's A minor nocturne for Flugelhorn and Viola?" I quipped.

The joke flew over Jacks head and disappeared towards the horizon.

"No, you soft bugger. It was 'When The Saints Go Marching In'." he said looking crestfallen.

He handed the dripping harmonica back to me and I carefully placed it in my pocket, vowing never to play it again.

"Anyway, I've got some information for you." he said bringing sheets of crumpled paper out of his pocket.

The previous day I had mentioned my interest in a particular type of sports watchstrap from America.

"I phoned the company last night for you and spoke to the CEO" he said.

He handed me the paper on which was a comprehensive list of trade prices, retail costs, sizes and colours, delivery times and import duties. This was typical Jack, supremely capable and never one to let the grass grow under his feet; Even if he did have moss between his toes.

"Thanks, Jack," I said rather taken aback at his forthrightness.

"It's all there lad, all the info you need. I keep telling you; learn from me while you can. You never know when I might breathe my last." He placed a hand on my shoulder, "I won't be here forever, you know."

"You're as fit as a flea," I said smiling.

"I'm as fit as two fleas," he snapped, "Not bad for nearly eighty am I?" An evil look came into his eyes and he pointed down towards his sagging crotch area. "Mind you," he smirked, "He's still only twenty-five!"

He suddenly turned on his heels and shouted over his shoulder "Watch this". He then took off at great speed through the car park, narrowly missing a departing icecream van. After twenty yards he turned and sprinted back towards me with a look of grim determination on his face.

"Not bad eh?" He said red in the face and panting heavily. "I've still got it!"

What it was he had still got, I hate to think. But whatever it was, it was now residing inside my harmonica, having a party and multiplying by the second.

One thing was certain; Jack had years left in him. There was still plenty of time left to learn...

***

Chapter 12

HOMEWARD BOUND

'You are as dead now as you ever will be.'

Seth

I didn't want to pick the phone up, but its persistent noise compelled me to. I didn't want to hear the news it might bring; I wasn't ready for it yet, but then, I never would be.

"Hello."

"Nick, it's Jacky." My heart missed a beat. Jacky is Dilly's older sister, and my head knew why she was calling, even though my heart told me otherwise.

"Nick, I'm so sorry. Dad didn't make it. He died about thirty minutes ago."

And that was it! A life finished in a phone call...the end of an era. The loss of a friendship that was precious to both him and me. But the real pain came from knowing that I had to tell Dilly that her father had died. The moment I had dreaded for ten years. Watching someone you love have their heart broken is painful beyond compare. I felt pretty useless. All I could do was hold her, knowing there was no way I could shield her from the hurt.

We had received a call earlier in the day to say that her father, Ron, had been taken to hospital. This was nothing new for him; we had been in this situation before, many times... It wasn't until we received another call in the afternoon to say he'd taken a turn for the worse that we became worried. We had packed the car in preparation for the three hundred mile dash to Dilly's parent's home. I had just sent the boys to go and sit in the car when the dreaded phone call had come. We had an emotionally fraught fifteen minutes to ourselves and then I fetched the boys into the house. They knew from the look on my face that something terrible had happened. Jim, the youngest at nine, cried immediately, whilst Sam at thirteen seemed shocked and bewildered.

Ron had been the most wonderful grandad, placid, soft, funny and gentle, like a goo- natured old bear. The kids always delighted in surprising him. Because we lived so far away, they didn't get to see their grandparents as often as they would have wished. When we did make visits, we always tried to do it without Ron knowing we were coming. We would arrive late at night after a five-hour journey, and the boys would enter the house first. They would both walk nonchalantly into the living room, as if they had just nipped down the shops for five minutes. Grandad, they knew, would be in his favourite chair, watching television. "Oh hi, Grandad," they would say as casually as possible. There would be a moment's silence whilst the news found its way to granddads brain. Once it hit the target he would erupt with delight and we would walk into the room to find granddad buried under two boys, with arms and legs sticking out everywhere, and kisses being planted on any available area of head, neck, foot or any other accessible surface.

I sat the boys down and tried to explain to them how it was time to let granddad go. For the last few years he had been trapped in a body that didn't work anymore. The best way I could explain it to the children was to liken his body to a car. The car had become old and rusty. Parts of the engine kept breaking and had to be replaced, the headlights were dim and it kept overheating. One day it broke down never to go again, but granddad, who was driving the car, climbed out, shut the door and walked off. He had now gone to have a bit of a rest from driving, but eventually he would go out and look for a new car to drive. It might be a different model, a fast sports car, or a slow cruiser, and the choice of colour would be down to granddad.

This sad news had come about six weeks into the New Year, and was the culmination of a tense few months. The previous November, Ron had been admitted into hospital after being diagnosed with mouth cancer. He endured a ten-hour operation to remove half his tongue, and had his throat cut full across to remove his lymph nodes.

After what seemed a lifetime, he was finally wheeled into the intensive care unit, where we were allowed a brief visit. He was drowsy, but still managed a feeble 'thumbs up' when he saw us.

Looking at him lying in bed, it was as if the curtain of time had been thrown open and I was looking back nine years previous to when we had all been in this situation before. On that occasion Ron had been in hospital to have an operation to remove a brain tumour. The initial procedure had been a success, but before long complications set in and Ron lapsed into a deep coma. He would regain consciousness briefly and then lapse back into unconsciousness for days on end. This continued for three months and was a terrifying roller coaster ride that none of us could climb off. Over those three months, he endured a further seven brain operations, and none of us were even sure if he would survive. And if he did survive, would he be brain damaged?

The scariest moment of all was when the nursing staff informed us that Ron had now also contracted meningitis. At that time I thought there was no way back for him. But he was a stubborn old sod and refused to go. He battled on, and we battled along with him, spending hours by his bedside talking to him when in one of his comatose moments, or spoon-feeding him when awake. I think many people, nursing staff included, had given him up for dead.

One very close family friend refused to come and visit, stating that he "wanted to remember him the way he was"! I can remember feeling so angry towards this person for voicing such an insensitive opinion.

However, other people hadn't counted on how tenacious Ron's family were. There was no way he was going anywhere without a fight. I remember one person summing them up perfectly, "When the shit hits the fan," she said, "Your family don't run for cover, you hold brollies over each other and carry on!"

Terrible situations can still be a valuable way of learning lessons. Myself, Dilly and her three sisters have all learned Reiki healing. I can remember sitting by Ron's hospital bed in the intensive care unit and holding his hand whilst administering some healing energy. Within seconds of starting, all the machines went haywire and alarms started to go off. This brought nurses sprinting to his bedside from all directions. They would quickly check him over, look puzzled and re set the machines, only to have the whole process repeated five minutes later. In the end I found it easier to do distant healing, where I wasn't actually by Ron's side.

Every night I would send him healing whilst meditating. At first it seemed quite a simple task, but after a while I found it harder and harder to relax my mind enough to allow the healing to come through. The intensity of the predicament seemed to prevent me from viewing the situation dispassionately. In short, I was trying too hard. I was trying to force the energy, and it was no longer working.

I came to realise that how I viewed the situation was up to me. It was my choice to decide how I felt, and that would determine the intensity of the healing. I decided it was time to use my sixth sense, my sense of humour! After all, I had tried everything else. This time I imagined Ron lying in his hospital bed, and in my minds eye I created the most enormous custard pie. But instead of a filling of sweet ambrosia nectar, I packed the pie to overflowing with healing energy. "Right, you're gonna get this one right in the kisser," I would say to myself before metaphorically throwing the pie fully into Ron's face. In my mind's eye I could see it hit him in the face with a satisfying SPLOSH! It covered him from head to toe in healing energy.

I know plenty of people reading this will accuse me of being a fruitcake, and having just read back what I've written, I can't say that I blame them, it does sound far fetched, but all I know is that it worked. As I ran these images through my head I could feel the energy surge through my hands, turbo-boosted. This soon became my nightly routine and the poor man had more pies thrown at him than a snotty child on Tiswas. In the interest of fairness though, I should state that the Spotted Dick realised very disappointing results.

Eventually, after months of unstinting care and attention from the family, he slowly started to recover. In the end he made a full recovery, with no long lasting effects, (other than a strange dent in the middle of his forehead about the size of a polo-mint) Miracles do happen, I have seen it!

You might think that that was enough medical drama for one lifetime. But not for Ron, who did like a good hospital! Over the next nine years there followed spells in hospitals in Spain, which necessitated an un-scheduled mercy flight home. There were also visits to numerous hospitals throughout Britain, with very few major cities escaping his scrutiny of their healthcare system. A broken arm, displaced shoulder, cataracts, gall stones, MRSA on countless occasions, liver failure and two strokes all came along in the next few years. It seemed that every few months the phone would ring to say that, once again, he had been rushed to hospital with yet another ailment. It became such a common occurrence that we made a joke out of them, and they became known as 'Ron's failed suicide attempts.'

And here we were again! Yet another intensive care unit...but this time something felt different. I looked at Ron lying in his bed with wires and monitors all around him, and the swollen stump of what had what once been his tongue looking like a piece of badly butchered meat. The stitches across his throat looked red raw and painful. There was still his 'thumbs up' and false bravado to shield his daughters from the trauma, but I detected something in his eyes that said he couldn't face any more trials. Quite simply, he had had enough.

Every once in a while we have moments of pure clarity in our life. Moments when the mist of emotions that clouds our judgment disperses for a brief period, and we see the world as it truly is. As I looked into Ron's eyes, something unusual happened to me. It felt as if my consciousness slipped from my body briefly, and I was no longer bound by the rules and constraints that a body imposes on thought. I have absolute conviction that we have a "higher self" that is a part of our soul that doesn't reside within our bodies, but exists in the spirit realm. It is simply a part of us that is another facet of our consciousness. I am certain that at that point, both Ron's and my own higher self were communicating. I told him that he didn't need to do this any more; that he didn't need to go through any more pain and fear. That if he got the chance to pass over, he should embrace it fully and to go back to where he came from and not to try and hang on for the rest of us. It may sound a strange statement to admit that you are happy to let someone die. But it is born out of a love for someone, and love is the most powerful energy in the universe. Far more powerful than the fear of losing someone, and more powerful than selfishly wanting him to hang on so I wouldn't have to deal with any pain or sorrow. I knew that he would be going to a better place; a place where he was no longer ill, a loving place, and a place that we all come from. How could I deny someone the trip of a lifetime? The trip home...

As always, Ron battled on; but something in his eyes told me that he didn't quite have the energy for another round of jabs, left hooks and taking it on the chin. After he came out of the intensive care unit he was placed on an ordinary ward, where within days the dreaded MRSA hit him yet again! This set his recovery back by another week, but as always, he rallied again.

However, this was Ron and hospitals, always an unsteady mix. His next trauma was self-inflicted. He cut his tongue whilst shaving! (Yes, you did read that correctly) Let me explain. When Ron concentrated, he always stuck his tongue out. Whether it was doing crosswords, hanging wallpaper, playing snooker, or any number of tasks that required a bit of thought, his tongue would always be visible. Shaving was a serious business to Ron, as he always wanted to look good for "his girls." So what had taken surgeons ten hours to do, Ron did with a single careless stroke of his 'mach three turbo,' and took a further slice off his already much diminished tongue.

As you can imagine, it bled profusely and had medical staff in a mild panic trying to stop the torrent. After fifteen minutes of trying, the blood was still flowing freely from Ron's mouth. A Bi-Polar machine was rushed into the room in an attempt to cauterise the wound, only to discover that none of the staff on duty had been trained to use it. Once again, step forward a family member to save the day. Ron's middle daughter, Debbie, had used this very machine when she trained at a nearby hospital. The panicky doctor asked her to quickly scrub up and get to work before her father bled to death. She did so, and saved her fathers life. This gave Ron even more pride in his daughters, who meant the world to him.

For the next fortnight he rode the hospital roller coaster of "getting better highs" and "Oh no, MRSA again lows". Eventually, he came home. But something was missing. (Not just half his tongue.) On every other occasion when he returned from hospital, he had a renewed vigour for life, a rekindled interest in everything. He was always desperate to get out and do things. Days out, short hotel breaks, even shopping! But this time was different. A part of him hadn't returned after the last operation. He was constantly tired and not a little grumpy; totally unheard of for this most placid of men. Everyday tasks seemed beyond him, and holding on to life seemed a constant battle. He struggled on for a few more weeks, but eventually the inevitable happened. The phone call of his death marked the end of a significant chapter in our lives, but it wasn't the end of the book.

Obviously, as a family we were all deeply affected, but almost within hours we came to realise that, in the end, it was simply his time to go; he had had enough, and a calm resignation descended over us all.

The news had come only two days after a significant moment in my own life. A few weeks earlier I had discovered a mysterious lump in the intimate area peculiar to men where there should only be two lumps. Dilly didn't seem unduly worried by my revelation and had taken to calling me ET (the Extra Testicle), which she, and all her friends, found highly amusing.

A trip to the doctors did nothing to erase my fears. He donned a rubber glove, had a good rummage around as though he were choosing fruit in Sainsbury's, and declared; "I think that's an epididimal cyst. It is perfectly harmless. However, I thought that about the last one I saw and that turned out to be cancer, so I think I'll send you for a scan just to be safe."

I left with the word *cancer* ringing in my ears. Dilly, who is one of life's optimists, kept reminding me that the doctor had also said it was a harmless cyst. I tried to concentrate on this, but when someone mentions cancer in a sentence to you, it's very hard to get it out of your mind.

My scan date was in a fortnight, which left me plenty of time to mull over my situation. I did at one point have a serious chat with myself over what I would do if my extra plum turned out to be cancerous. The thought of dying didn't bother me too much, but I did give serious consideration as to what would happen to Dilly and the boys. Would they be financially secure without me, or would they have to sell up and move house? I would miss the boys growing up, getting married and having children of their own. And could I face invasive surgery, or chemotherapy? I kept all these thoughts to myself; after all, there was no need to worry anyone else about them. They didn't take up a great deal of my time, but they were issues that might need addressing. Needles to say I waited with baited breath and clenched buttocks for the scan.

And so it came to pass that I found myself lying on my back, legs akimbo, naked from the waist down whilst a stranger wearing rubber gloves fondled my gentlemen vegetables. "People pay a fortune for this in Bangkok," I said, " And here I am in good old Cornwall getting it done for free." The doctor gave me a tired look that said, *Son, I get these comments every day, and I'm just doing my job.* I was only trying to cover my nerves, using humour to deflect my apprehension. I decided it might be wise to keep quite from here on in, lest he give an extra squeeze. After all, I was in no position to argue. He held all the aces, so to speak!

He applied some freezing cold jelly, held the scanner to the appropriate area and stared intently at the monitor.

"Epididimal cyst!" he declared emphatically. "It's perfectly harmless. Now pull your trousers up."

I was so relieved that I all but told him I loved him and would he like to marry me.

"Don't let anyone near you with a scalpel!" he said.

He didn't need to tell me that, it's a rule I've lived by for years. That and, never dance the CanCan in a paddling pool in your wife's stilettos.

His parting shot showed that he did have a sense of humour. "If it gets so big you start tripping over it, come back and see me."

I left feeling like a new man. After all, I was special. Most men only had two. Some poor devils only had one, but not me. I, the chosen one, had three. I kept telling Dilly that she didn't know how lucky she was, and did she fancy a game of pocket billiards?

I won't bore you with her reply.

***

Jack Bell and I had been discussing 'Old Blue Eyes.' I had asked Jack whom he considered to be the ultimate entertainer.

"Sinatra was the best ever," he stated with conviction. "Perfect pitch, perfect phrasing, and a unique tonal quality to his voice, delivered with charisma – best ever by a mile. I met him once, a friend of mine got me and my wife back stage and we watched from the wings as he sang his final number. As he came off my mate introduced us. 'Mr Sinatra,' he said, 'this is Jack Bell and his wife, Jack used to play with Maynard Fergusson.' He were a proper gentleman, he said some nice things about Maynard's music and shook my hand warmly and gave my wife a kiss on the cheek. Nicky lad, you should have seen her face, it were magical." And just for that moment, I knew by looking in his eyes that Jack was no longer standing with me. He was miles away and years ago, reliving a treasured moment. I think he may have been genuinely star-struck. That had never happened before. He'd always considered himself the equal of anybody, he wasn't impressed by rank or fortune, he was a 'Yorkshire lad' and therefore, as good as, if not better than the next man. I think he viewed Mr Sinatra differently, reverentially and a little bit sacred. I believe Jack respected genius when he saw it.

"He gave my wife a signed photo" Jack said, "It stayed on her dressing table till the day she died." His voice trailed away sadly, as his mind came back to the present day.

"I attended Sinatra's funeral, you know."

"You went to Frank Sinatra's funeral?" I asked, astounded, "How on earth did that come about?"

"I was asked to go as a representative of Armand Zildjian, who couldn't attend." he explained. "There was a special guest list, and I had to give my name to two security guards, who checked it off a list. I got there early to make sure I had a good seat. They were all there you know, Liza Minnelli, Kirk Douglas, Tony Bennett, Jack Nicholson, Gregory Peck, there were hundreds of 'em."

Jack was telling me this impressive tale as strawberry juice dribbled down his chin. He had arrived with a punnet in his hand earlier that morning. My eldest son, Sam, then aged 4, was at work with me for the day, and he was only too happy to sit with Jack and help him eat the strawberries. It was lovely to see Jack's reaction to dealing with a small child. Gone was the loud voice; gone was the contradiction of anything you said. The brash and forthright attitude had disappeared and in its place was a quiet, friendly, open manner. He sat for a long while talking to my son, but it wasn't in that condescending way that some people use with small children; he spoke to him on the same level. Kids of that age haven't yet learned the art of judging *people by their appearance, and Sam and Jack spent a happy hour discussing nonsense and eating strawberries.*

At one time, Jack and Maynard Fergusson had gone into business together manufacturing trumpets and Jack always carried a Fergusson-Bell mouthpiece in his pocket. He took it out and blew a few notes from it. Sam looked on enchanted, not only did this man have strawberries; he could also make impressively rude noises with his hand. He became an instant hero.

Jack was full of excitement this day. He was due to fly out to Florida in the next week; it was his favourite part of the world. For the last few months he had talked about going back there, as he thought it would probably be his last chance to see it. He had a boyish, end-of-term look about him. At one point, he'd even asked me if I'd go with him as his companion, even offering to pay my airfare. Of course I declined, with a wife and two small children at home, I could hardly go jetting off to Florida for three months. However, I might have been able to stop him loading up his Winnebago to the roof with cheese.

Before he left, Jack made sure I had his mobile phone number so that we could keep in touch. I left it a week before ringing to make sure he was settled in – there was no answer, so I left a message. The next week I received a postcard with a picture on the front of an island paradise on Florida's west coast. Jack had written

This place is equal to if not better than, the West Indies, the Seychelles, Mauritius and all the other places in the world that millions rush off to. I am living in the historical fishing village of Cortez on Anna-Maria Island, a gem in the ocean or should I say the Gulf of Mexico. Many thanks for the voicemail message.

P.S. Tell your boy the strawberries are the best in the world

Two days after receiving the postcard, I had a phone call to tell me that Jack had died. Looking back, I think Jack perhaps knew that he didn't have long, and I find it comforting to think of him spending his last few days somewhere that he loved, where he was warm and happy, near the ocean and in sunshine. It seemed a fitting end and far more respectful than being found huddled up in a tumbled down caravan in a distant corner of a windswept field.

When I think back over the time we spent together I cherish the memories I have of him. He was such a strong character; he could be both infuriating and charming at the same time. He taught me not to judge people on their appearance alone, and to try to see the inner person. What had started out on my part as an inconvenience, with this smelly old loony coming to see me, soon developed into a friendship with a man old enough to have been my grandfather. I realised that if I looked beyond the stained clothes, there was a really interesting, charismatic person. Here was someone who lived a full and eventful life and was more than willing to share it with you – warts and all. (The warts stories would fill a book on their own, but believe me; they would never pass censorship and indecency laws.)

Jack was just another person who has come in and out of my life, but he left his mark – a greasy thumbprint on my forehead.

***

Chapter 13

GOOD VIBRATIONS

I'm vibrating at the speed of light.

Take my hand we'll light up the night

REM

With the death of my father in law, my mind was cast back all those years ago, to when I was a small boy and my granddad had died. My feelings were the same now; sadness at his passing, but somewhere deep inside a belief that it wasn't "all over." I still reasoned that once something was *made*, it couldn't suddenly be *unmade*; to totally not exist in any form whatsoever; that would seem to go against everything I had learned.

As before, I thought about the 'observer' that looked at the world through Ron's eyes. I had learned enough to know that it hadn't just disintegrated with his passing.

Quantum physics holds the key to explaining about the observer in us all. In the film/documentary *"What the bleep do we know?"* Dr Fred Alan Wolf PhD explained about the "observer" and how science has looked for it in every part of the brain. It can't find it. It's not there. There is no part of the brain that is the "observer" looking out. The brain can be wired up to high tech machines to show which parts of the brain light up when you are thinking, but it can't show you where those thoughts originated or what creates them. So if thought isn't created within the brain, it must mean that it is created outside of the brain in a matter-free dimension, and then "projected" into it in order to create an illusion of reality. In effect, the brain is the hard drive information receptor that our thoughts are beamed into. This means that the "observer" lives outside of our bodies in a matter-free world, a world of pure thought. Dare we call that world 'the spirit world'?

For thousands of years we thought the atom was the smallest thing in the world. We were told it was like a small hard ball and that it was the building block on which all matter is formed. Then we split the atom and discovered that we were wrong. We now know that an atom is made up of billions of sub atomic particles, and quite a lot of empty space. The interesting thing is that quantum physics has discovered that these particles have the ability to appear and disappear. They seem able to pop in and out of existence. This is called Quantum Particle Positioning. This begs the question, where do these particles go when they are not here? Do they go into a parallel universe?

Dr Wolf suggests that we should not look upon these particles as "things", but as tendencies or possibilities, like thought. They aren't solid and they have the ability to pop in and out of reality, and you and I are made up of these things, billions and billions of them, all vibrating together to form the creation of us. But not only us, the chair that I am sitting on, the pen I am using to write this, all the plants, rocks and grass in my garden, the earth itself, the universe and everything that is in it , are all just bits of matter vibrating in and out of reality. At the sub atomic level, all matter is the same and it is all interconnected. We are literally made up of particles that come in and out of our reality. So if we consider these particles as thoughts or tendencies, then that means we are 'made' out of pure thoughts. This in turn must mean that our natural state is as spiritual beings who live in a matter-free world. We think we are our bodies, but we aren't; we are spiritual beings who use our bodies as a tool to carry our consciousness in order to manifest reality, so that we may learn from our experiences.

Buddha said that *it is your mind that creates this world.* And I believe that that is what we do. We use our brain to create situations that we can relate or react to. In the film, Professor Amit Goswami PhD explains this:

"We all have a habit of thinking that everything around us is already a thing, existing without my input, without my choice. You have to banish that kind of thinking. Instead you have to recognise that the material world around us, the chairs, the tables, the room, and the carpet, all of these are nothing but possible movements of my consciousness. And I am choosing moment by moment, to bring my actual experience into manifestation. This is the only radical thinking that you need to do, but it is so radical. It's so difficult; because our tendency is that the world is already out there, independent of my experience. It is not. Heisenberg himself, co-discoverer of Quantum Physics, said atoms are not things. They are only tendencies. So, instead of thinking of things, you have to think of possibilities...possibilities of consciousness."

So to the age-old question, *why are we here?* Answer; to learn! We choose to incarnate in order to learn lessons. We might choose to learn about love, or hate, or happiness, or prejudice, or any infinite number of things. And we learn from other people by interacting with them, for at our deepest level, WE ARE ALL ONE, all inter-connected. This is clarified in the film *What the Bleep Do We Know:*

"I am my atoms, but I am also my cells. I am also my macroscopic physiology. It's all true. They're just different levels of truth. The deepest level of truth uncovered by science and by philosophy is the fundamental truth of unity. At the deepest sub nuclear level of our reality, you and I are literally one." John Hagelin PhD.

Dr Stuart Hameroff puts it another way: "Knowing that there is this interconnectedness of the universe, that we are all interconnected and that we are connected to the universe at its fundamental level, I think is as good an explanation for spirituality as there is."

At our most fundamental level we are a collection of atoms and cells, bundles of energy, vibrating at the speed of light to create *us*, all of us, and every living thing on the planet. Oh yes, and the planet as well, and the whole universe, are all interconnected. We share a unifying force that bonds all of creation together. We are quite literally all made from the same *stuff*, irrespective of creed, colour or religion; we are all part of the whole, 'All That Is'

I've never bought into the idea of God being an old man with a big white beard who sits around in heaven choosing who to save and who to cast into eternal damnation. I believe in some kind of Supreme Being or universal consciousness, but I should imagine that it is so far out of my ability to comprehend that I don't even try. Perhaps this interconnectedness is all part of God, and we are all the fundamental particles that make up God.

Fred Alan Wolf, PhD., to the rescue again: "I have no idea what God is. Yet, I have this experience that God is. There is something very real about this presence called God, although I have no idea how to define God, to see God as a person or a thing. I can't seem to do it. Asking a human being to explain what God is, is like asking a fish to explain the water in which the fish swims."

We know that thought/consciousness manifests itself physically as electronic signals in the brain, but we know the brain doesn't create it. We also know that energy is indestructible, it never dies. So where does this consciousness go when it no longer has a brain to reveal itself through?

Answer, it returns to the dimension from whence it originated, a place outside of our three dimensional realm of existence. We can't see it or touch it, but that doesn't mean it isn't real. We live in a narrow band of reality, and only perceive what our senses allow us to. We are slaves to them in a way, but there is plenty of 'stuff' out there that goes on without us perceiving it. For instance, blow a dog whistle and you hear nothing, but within seconds every dog in the neighbourhood should come running to your feet. They hear it because they have a different hearing range to humans. Similarly, take the visible light spectrum. This is the amount of light/colour that our eyes can perceive. We see this through an electromagnetic waveband. Each colour has its own wavelength, the longest wavelength we see is the colour red and the length decreases through the spectrum of orange, yellow, green, blue, indigo, to violet which has the shortest wavelength. (This is also the sequence and colours of the chakras, or energy centres, throughout the body.) But there is also infra- red and ultra-violet which lies outside of our sight which we also know is there. Just because we can't see it, doesn't mean it doesn't exist

Or, look at it this way. Imagine that we live our lives in a long corridor. We were born in the corridor, and everything that we know of exists in that corridor with us. There are no windows, but there are doors. We spend our life walking down the corridor and we open some of the doors as we go. We take a look inside and see new wonders or meet new people or have new experiences with every door that is opened. We spend our whole life within its walls; thinking that this is all there is to reality. Eventually, we get to the end of the corridor and we die. Our consciousness floats out of our body and we start to move away. We can look back and see the 'shell', or body, that housed our consciousness for a short while. Gradually, we float further and further away and we suddenly realise that we are floating outside of the corridor, and from our vantage point we see that the corridor was actually just a small section of a huge building, all with millions of corridors disappearing into infinity, one above another. We were only on the second floor and we never realised there was so much more to see. Occasionally we may have heard some strange noises coming from above us. It might have been voices or footsteps, but whenever we said anything to anyone else they would say, "Don't be stupid! That's just your imagination.

Can you see another corridor? Ours is the only one that exists!"

The realisation that at our deepest level we are all part of a universal consciousness, and knowing that we are all incarnated to learn lessons, had made me realise something profound. I had always thought of my life as two separate parts. One part was a strange spiritual quest for answers, and the other was my work life, and I always considered them separate and distinct. Nothing could be further from the truth! I now realise that some of people I have met through my work have taught me just as much as anything I could have found in a book.

I have learned about how I view other people, how I view the world, and about how I view myself. I have learned about joy, anger, laughter, empathy, pity, (revulsion on the odd occasion) and a million other things.

I've met young, old, happy, sad, black, white and every colour in-between, (especially sunburnt red in august) local, foreign, different planet!

There was George, the man who told me of his horrific experience during the war, when he was one of the first soldiers to liberate Belsen concentration camp; and Olga, the huge 'bottle blonde' Russian drilling engineer, who wanted to steal me away to Vladivostok; There was the lady, who only last week, berated me for being a devil worshipper, and informed me that God had sent her to save me.

Only a short while ago I had the pleasure of meeting a pair of twin boys from Russia. Two happy smiling faces beamed out from beneath two overly large baseball caps. They looked to be around my youngest son's age. Their English was very limited, so I chatted to the person they were with. He explained that he was a charity volunteer who dealt with children from Chernobyl. These two young boys were orphans whose parents had died of cancer after the nuclear disaster. The charity was involved in giving children the opportunity of a holiday. The twins were in remission after their own battles with the disease.

I have been reduced to tears on a number of occasions. One elderly gentleman told me of the time he spent in the war. He recounted how he had been on patrol in the desert of North Africa. Whilst driving across the vast expanse of wasteland, he and a comrade had come across a lone British military truck that had been attacked and destroyed. There was only one survivor, a young boy of around seventeen years of age. He died in the gentleman's arms calling for his mother. The image of that young man haunted me for years, and from my safe and secure vantage point I can only imagine the horror that that poor boy went through. To die in the arms of a stranger calling for your mum seems as good an example of the futility of war that I can think of.

I've met Harry 'the bomb', a feisty 80-year-old Normandy Landings Veteran, Chris 'the cake' whose baps are the finest in Cornwall, and Surja, the retired doctor who brings me back fresh tea from his family's plantation in India. I've recently met two jackpot lottery winners who were down in Cornwall house hunting. And quite literally, tens of thousands of people all with a unique story to tell.

I've realised that one of my major life lessons has been trying not to judge people on appearance alone. This is quite a tricky one because we all subconsciously size people up without thinking about it. We make an instant judgement based on their appearance. I have had numerous examples of this where I have instantly 'pigeon-holed' a customer into a distinct category, only to be proved wrong almost instantly. Jack Bell being a prime example. He could be described as being dirty, scruffy, self opinionated, brash, and prone to dribbling down his shirtfront. But overriding all of that was the immense force of personality that was Jack; amusing, knowledgeable, ebullient, fun loving, and painfully honest.

Edward Lloyd was another man who taught me a valuable lesson in not judging by appearance. I first met Edward when he was in his mid seventies. He had suffered from cancer of the mouth that had left him severely facially disfigured. A huge operation had left him with no tongue or pallet to his mouth and his cheeks had had so much flesh removed that they where virtually non existent, leaving his face with a skeletal appearance which was quite shocking at first sight. His speech was severally impaired due to the lack of a tongue. It took me a while to understand him, but the more I got to know him the easier it became. It wasn't long before Edward's appearance was forgotten as the strength of his personality shone through. We became great friends and I spent many happy hours at his home chatting with him and his lovely wife Kay, to the point that they felt more like family than friends.

Edward had led an extraordinary life. He was a world-renowned metallurgist and had spent the war years working on some extraordinary projects. He assisted Barnes Wallis in the development of the Bouncing Bomb, worked on the invention of Radar, and was instrumental in the creation of the jet engine - and he still found time to serve on the Olympic Financial Committee with Prince Phillip. However, Edward's first love had always been music, and he played the organ to a professional standard.

During the war he also organised troop entertainment and it was in this capacity that he met and became friends with Glen Miller, even managing to play in his band on a few occasions. This was more than just a casual acquaintance, as the two men became good friends, and Glen Miller actually had dinner with Edward and Kay only two days before he disappeared.

Edward was a very modest man and his stories were never given in a boastful manner. They almost had to be coaxed out of him, unlike Jack Bell who told you whether you wanted to know or not! I treasured the friendship that I shared with Edward and he taught me, above anyone else I have ever met, the importance of not judging a book by its cover.

I can still remember the last time I saw him. I had been to visit, as he had been unwell, and as I was leaving he stood up, gripped me firmly by the hand and looked me in the eyes. "Thank you so much for being my friend," he said, and I could tell from the look on his face that he truly meant it. He died a week later, at home, surrounded by his loving family.

That such a man considered me his friend was an honour, and I felt humbled by his kind words. At the time, he was well into his eighties, but friendship has no boundaries by age. And here he was thanking me for our friendship, when it should have been me thanking him.

I realised that reading all the books in the world couldn't have given me as valuable a lesson as Edward taught me. Sitting quietly and meditating is a wonderful thing to do, and very valuable in a lot of areas of my life, but you also have to remember to get involved with life, not just watch from the sidelines. And this is where my time spent at market and meeting thousands of different people has been invaluable. My two lives haven't been separate at all; my interactions with other people have taught me just much as any séance or having my aura photographed. And although I've explored past lives to discover all that I have been, it's important to remember that I have a foot in this world as well, and the opportunity to be all that I can be now. It's all part of the same journey.

And it's the same journey that we are all making, every one of us. It's a journey where we interact with each other. We all affect the world around us, insofar as what we think, say or do, directly affects those around us, seen or unseen by ourselves. It places the burden of responsibility fairly and squarely on our own shoulders and makes us realise the inescapable truth of the laws of cause and effect.

This didn't just occur to me of course. There has been no sudden imparting of astral wisdom, bought about by serving the old man in the flat cap with a watch that smelt of toilets. No, this was something that had crept up on me over the years. Concepts such as Life After Death, Re-incarnation, and Parallel Universes etc, are so diverse and difficult to comprehend, that it took a long while for the 'drip –drip' effect of information to sink in. As the years rolled by they became cemented in my mind as totally plausible. As I had reasoned before when attending the New

Age Fayre, it's unreasonable to sit under some dodgy pipework in the shape of a pyramid and expect the answers of the universe to be conveyed to you in one blinding flash of illumination. You have to put in the groundwork. In the end, *it's the journey that's important, not the destination.*

It is a shame that this wasn't all conveyed to me as a child though. It would have been so much more convenient to have had all of this imparted to me in the blinding flash of a cosmic visitation. Saving me years of research and a small fortune in books. I had even worked out how it would happen. As a boy I had imagined it down to the last detail;

I would be awoken from my childlike slumber by a strange light filling the room. The sweet sound of a heavenly choir would be heard singing quietly in the background. There would be the tinkle of bells, chiming as softly as droplets of water falling into a crystal-clear pool. The strange light would grow stronger and stronger, increasing in intensity. There would be a sound of distant thunder, and then a strange mist would materialise, and through the haze there would appear a mercurial figure (a bit like *Stars in their Eyes*). He would be a figure of immense power and authority around 7ft tall. He would be adorned in shimmering robes, have flowing silver hair and a long white beard. He would stare down at me from his great height, with piercing blue eyes that looked as it they held fire behind them – he would peer into my very soul.

"BEHOLD, I AM HERE!" He would proclaim in a voice louder than Brian Blessed's. The room would echo like a great cathedral, his voice bouncing off the walls. In his powerful hands he would carry a gnarled wooden staff, which he would point at my body shaking and quivering under the covers.

"STOP THAT YOU DIRTY DEVIL, IT WILL SEND YOU BLIND, NOW PUT YOUR HANDS WHERE I CAN SEE THEM." He would spread his arms wide. "I AM JEHAZOQIM! (Why are these powerful figures always called by such fabulous names? Whatever happened to Archangel Kevin?) I AM A LIGHT LORD OF THE SEVENTH REALM, AND I COME TO YOU TODAY TO IMPART GREAT KNOWLEDGE. BECAUSE YOU MY CHILD..." here he would pause for dramatic effect, "ARE THE CHOSEN ONE." He would drop onto one knee and bow his head in supplication as lightening bolts danced around the room. I would play it cool,

"Come, come," I would say modestly, "you must have the wrong man, little old me, the chosen one? Get away with you," I would utter, with a chuckle and a dismissive wave of my hand. But of course, I knew really that I *was* the chosen one, that I *was* different to everyone else. I'd known it all my life, which was why no one ever wanted to play with me as a child. Other kids recognised my greatness and were scared by it. I realised that their cries of 'weirdo' were just cries of endearment.

I had my disciples, hundreds of kids would follow me all over our local estate, and they would shout after me and throw offerings, like rocks, pebbles and plastic bottles. I had to play down my greatness. I used to have to pretend to be bad at football for fear of my skills embarrassing them. I always took it in good grace when the kid with glasses and callipers was picked before me. I didn't mind being the last one chosen. I'd always been taught 'ladies first', and to be fair, some of the girls chosen before me could actually kick the ball without falling over. I never turned a hair when there was just 'Bobby' the Jack Russell and myself left to pick - I fully understood them wanting the dog. He was quite quick, even if he did regularly eat the ball and cock his leg up the goal posts – but then most of the boys did as well.

Anyway, their thin veneer of pretence, that they didn't recognise my greatness, slipped occasionally, "You've got 'im!" the opposing captain would say with a sneer pointing at me. Everyone would turn to look at me standing alone on the goal line, dressed in a pair of my dads old shorts, with two matchstick legs protruding from them, wearing my Dunlop 'green flash' trainers that were so full of holes my socks pocked through the soles; Sporting a 'plop brown' jumper made by my granny, with the unique feature of mittens actually knitted into the sleeves, my 'home haircut' making me look like I'd been butchered with a Flymo, and a thin dribble of syrupy snot sliding cautiously out of my left nostril; I would be smiling wanly...

"Oh God!" my teammates would cry.

You see...? They did know really.

THE OMEGA...

Whenever I think of Jack Bell, an image runs through my head of him at Frank Sinatra's funeral. I can see him now, tapping a weeping Liza Minnelli on the shoulder and offering her his handkerchief; a ragged piece of sackcloth with something akin to old cornflakes encrusted to it.

"Ere you are love," he'd say, "Have a good blow on that. Don't worry about me, I'll use me sleeve!"

In memory of
Jack Bell and Nipper...

Made in the USA
Charleston, SC
31 March 2016